THE ENGLISHMAN'S WATCH

By the same author:

An Irish Sea Cruising Guide (1976), Adlard Coles
A Cruising Guide to Anglesey and the Menai Strait (1977), James Laver, Liverpool
A Yachtsman's Navigation, in press
A Cruising Guide to the Isle of Man, in preparation

The classical fusee lever centre seconds chronograph, complete with a much worn silver link-and-fetter chain and a medallion. The movement is not named — either Coventry or more likely Prescot made. Key wound and hand setting by key. The stop button slide is to be seen at two o'clock. The sweep hand registers on an outer chapter showing three hundred fifths of a second. Case dated Chester 1881. *(Photograph by Ken Gatwood.)*

The Englishman's Watch

by

ROBERT KEMP

ALTRINCHAM
JOHN SHERRATT AND SON LTD

First published in 1979 by
John Sherratt and Son Ltd.,
78 Park Road, Altrincham

© 1979 Robert Kemp

ISBN 0 85427 052 3

Made and printed in England by
T. Stephenson & Sons Ltd Prescot Merseyside
and bound by John Sherratt and Son Ltd., Manchester

Contents

	Author's Note	11
1.	The Watch Collector Today	13
2.	The Swiss Watch	16
3.	The Waltham Pocket Watch	22
4.	The Rise of the Wristlet Watch	36
5.	The "Going Barrel" English Lever Watch	39
6.	The Centre-seconds Chronograph	45
7.	The English Fusee Lever	48
8.	The Verge	55
9.	The Nineteenth-century Verge	57
10.	The Later Eighteenth-century Verge	65
11.	The Early Eighteenth-century Verge	71
12.	The Rarer Escapements	73
13.	Leverization	82
14.	Regulation	85
15.	Pocket Watch Cases	89
16.	The Recased Watch	100
17.	The Dress Watch and the Goliath	104
18.	Pocket Watch Accessories	107
19.	The Provenance of a Watch	112
20.	Restoring a Watch	122
21.	Collecting Watches	127
22.	The Massacre of the Watches	134
23.	The Analysis	139
24.	Horological Literature	142
	Index	145

Illustrations

Frontispiece   A centre seconds Chronograph
1   A modern Swiss pocket watch
2   A Swiss movement
3   Dial of a watch signed William Bent of London
4   Movement of watch by Bent
5   Two characteristic Waltham watches
6   Waltham seven-jewel Traveller watch
7   Waltham fifteen-jewel watch
8   Waltham seventeen-jewel watch
9   Waltham seventeen-jewel Royal movement
10   Waltham seventeen-jewel P. S. Bartlett movement
11   Waltham nineteen-jewel Riverside movement
12   Waltham twenty-three-jewel Vanguard movement
13   Waltham twenty-three-jewel Riverside Maximus movement
14   Three older Waltham movements
15   Three Waltham movements
16   An early key wind Elgin
17   Top plate of movement of Elgin watch
18   Elgin twenty-one-jewel movement
19   Hamilton seventeen-jewel movement
20   Classic English lever, *c.*1890
21   Back of English lever
22   English lever from the Lancashire Watch Co.
23   Pair of watches, case-dated Birmingham 1898 and 1899
24   English lever by Benson
25   English lever by Penlington and Batty
26   Three-quarter plate lever by Henry Nalson
27   English lever by R. C. Oldfield
28   An unusually large and heavy piece
29   Flyback chronograph

30 Fusee lever by John Chesworth of Prescot
31 Demi-hunter cased centre-seconds chronograph
32 Top plate of Kellie watch
33 Dial of watch by John Kellie of Liverpool
34 Chronograph by J. Hargreaves of Liverpool
35 Top plate of Hargreaves watch
36 Centre-seconds watch by Pearce of Leeds
37 Chronograph by W. Samuel of Manchester
38 Fusee lever case-dated Birmingham 1890
39 Fusee lever by E. Meyer of Manchester
40 Fusee lever by T. R. Russell of Liverpool
41 Fusee lever by William Rowley of Liverpool
42 Dial of William Rowley watch
43 Fusee lever by Richard Thelwell of Manchester
44 Early fusee lever dial
45 Fusee lever by Savoury and Son, Cornhill, London
46 Fusee by Hester Mason of Liverpool
47 Verge by J. Jarvis of Whitchurch
48 Movement of Jarvis watch
49 Painted dial mid-nineteenth-century verge
50 Verge by Thos. Mawkes of Derby
51 Movement of Mawkes watch
52 Dial of demi-hunter verge in single consular case
53 Demi-hunter verge by J. Newton of London
54 Verge by Matthew Hick of York
55 Nineteenth-century verge
56 Dial of verge by Richard Ward of London
57 Dust cover of Ward watch
58 Movement of Ward watch
59 Typical eighteenth-century verge
60 Verge by John Hilton of London
61 Dial of eighteenth-century verge by Robert Innes of London
62 Eighteenth-century verge with "beetle and poker" hands
63 Verge by Grayhurst of London
64 Verge by Bartholomew Davis of Preston
65 Inner case and movement of Davis watch
66 Inner cases and dials of two mid-eighteenth-century verges
67 Three movements from the first half of the eighteenth century

68 Dust cover on an eighteenth-century verge
69 Fine verge by Archibald Coats of Wigan
70 Recased movement by Ric. Gibbs of London
71 Verge by Thos. Worswick of Lancaster
72 Verge by Rt. Barker of Liverpool
73 Verge by Edw. Fairclough of Liverpool
74 Verge by Geo. Booth of Manchester
75 French verge by Ballion of Paris
76 Top plate of French watch
77 Unusual skeleton verge probably by Joseph Finney of Liverpool
78 Verge by Edn. Cooper of London
79 Dial of Cooper watch
80 Top plate of Cooper watch
81 Side view of Cooper movement
82 Cylinder escapement by George Wilson of London
83 Cylinder movement by Wm. Seymour of London
84 Cylinder movement by W. and T. Baird of London
85 French or Swiss cylinder movement
86 Dial of rack lever watch by Litherland and Co. of Liverpool
87 Top plate of Litherland watch
88 Three Litherland movements
89 Rack lever by Robt. Roskell of Liverpool
90 Rack lever by Lister of Newcastle-on-Tyne
91 Two movements of the Ormskirk or clubfoot type
92 Clubfoot verge by Jas. Houghton of Ormskirk
93 Duplex movements by Thos. Earnshaw of London
94 Top plate of Earnshaw duplex
95 Dial of duplex watch by Grimalde and Johnson of London
96 Top plate of Grimalde and Johnson duplex
97 Three eighteenth-century verges
98 Massey lever escapement by Jas. Cornwall of Liverpool
99 Massey lever watch by F. J. Massey of Clerkenwell
100 Typical demi-hunter case from the 1920's
101 Engine-turning on the back of a good quality English case
102 Tortoiseshell covered outer case of an eighteenth-century verge

103 Shagreen covered outer case of an eighteenth-century verge
104 Typical marks on the back of a watch case
105 Markings inside a rolled gold case
106 Rolled gold guarantee inside the dome of a case
107 Monogram on a gold watch case
108 Long-service inscription on a gold watch
109 Watch paper
110 Watch "paper" with a sentimental verse
111 Watchmaker's advertisement
112 Watchmaker's advertisement
113 Watch paper
114 Piece of embroidery overlaying a watch paper
115 Embroidered memento for a watch case
116 Liverpool jewellery in a movement by Richard Pickford
117 Liverpool jewellery by William Bellion
118 Liverpool jewellery in a movement by James Hornby
119 Some tools for the watch collector
120 Commonplace watch keys
121 Three Birch universal keys
122 Two watch fobs
123 Dress watch chains
124 Leather watch guards
125 Double Albert chain
126 Single Albert chain
127 Massive single Albert chain
128 Prize sporting medallions
129 Fusee lever watch with Albert chain and medallion
130 Victorian woven horsehair watch guard
131 Simple boxwood bedside watchstand
132 Movement of a Swiss Automaton
133 Two dress watches
134 Engine-turned travelling watch case
135 Goliath travelling watch-clock in a silver case
136 Goliath travelling watch-clock in a silver case
137 Travelling case open to show Goliath watch-clock
138 Mr. R. E. Phillips
139 Mr. Stanley Smith

Author's Note

THE watches and movements described and illustrated here are, with one exception, from the author's personal collection, which for security reasons is not kept at the author's home.

The book describes the pieces, and builds up the background from which they sprang when they first found their way into the pockets of the people of this country. This is the first attempt to bring to the watch collector of today detailed information of the commonplace everyday watches which is so scarce in the standard texts.

An author can but guess at the technical standing of the potential reader of his book. He does know, however, that a book such as this is aimed at readers who come to it with some background of horology, meaning to build on this as they move to further fields as their collection grows. It would be invidious then to try to define commonplace terms. In the field of the older pocket watches these names have remained unchanged for centuries and have grown from the craft practices of the watchmakers. When he was trying to write a glossary to his book *Practical Watch Repairing*, Donald de Carle found that his list was expanding into another volume as big as the original book. He therefore published this as his *Watch and Clock Encyclopedia,* originally in 1950 with the latest edition in 1975. Rather than make parallel attempts here to define and re-define terms it seems far better for the student to use de Carle's *Encyclopedia* which is in itself a mine of background knowledge. In previous years F. J. Britten undertook the same task in his book *The Watch and Clock Makers' Handbook, Dictionary and Guide*. It was reproduced in facsimile in 1976. The first edition is dated 1884, and it is thus particularly appropriate for those collecting watches of this period. My own edition is the ninth—1896.

Colour photography for the dust jacket has been carried out by my friend Mr. Ken Gatwood. The black and white illustrations have been photographed, processed and enlarged by the author.

1
The Watch Collector Today

EXACTLY what does a man think he is doing in assembling a collection of old watches? Officially, and for the record, he is fascinated by the saga of portable time, the expertise of the old makers and the enslavement of man by his watch. Unconsciously there are so many other motives at work that it would need another book to explain why a collector collects. As my own hoard grew it became increasingly clear that the aims of such an exercise needed appraisal. Mere acquisitiveness cannot be an end in itself. At some stage it must be explained, justified or convincingly excused. While it is true that old watches and clocks have a fascination of their own the only real and natural aim of bringing them together is to show them to others. Such an exhibition would not only display the gems of the older craftsmen but also show the changes through which the watch has passed to reach the precision of today. In today's climate, however, such a showing would be unsafe outside a well-guarded museum—indeed my own specimens have to spend their life in a safe deposit rather than in the house. This is more than a pity, for everyone including myself is deprived of the pleasure of handling them "in the flesh". The only reasonable remaining alternative is to write and illustrate a book, and this is my excuse for having done so.

It is specifically written for the modest collector of today, working under the difficulties of scarcity and high prices that obtain now. In the past horology was a field in which the moneyed and cultured man could find exquisite pieces; with the result that these are now in private collections or museums and available in the market only to the serious investor. On the whole, however, really expensive watches reach their price level by reason of the case, but the movements of prestige makers are also to be found in cheap cases (or without any case at all) to suit the less wealthy client. It is my intention, therefore, to write about the unpretentious watch and particularly about the commonplace workaday watch of each historical period. The emphasis will naturally fall on the nineteenth and early twentieth century though most of the eighteenth century will be well represented. It will become clear that the writer is no more than an amateur, both as a horologist and a technician. It is hoped, however, to pass on to other amateurs experience gained in building up a collection large enough to cover the practical points of each period in watch development and design.

There is no real scarcity of books about the classical and traditional watch in use in this country at various times. The bibliography listed in Chapter 24 is simply that of books in my own library, and in these can be found more extensive lists of reference. It must be said, however, that these excellent texts concentrate on the older periods. Starting with the very beginning of recorded time, they continue animated and informed through the eighteenth century, but soon after the beginning of the nineteenth century the momentum is lost and the story stops abruptly. As a result the reader finds the last hundred years of the pocket watch almost undocumented so that many of his queries about his more recent and more mundane finds go unanswered. The lost hundred years extends from 1830 to the demise of the pocket watch about 1930. We are today separated from the time that every Englishman carried a pocket watch by a clear gap of forty to fifty years. This gives us a fairly precise start-line from which it is possible to work backwards into the centuries during which carried time developed. Admittedly to move from the modern to the more antique is a reversal of the usual historical sequence. It is, however, much more practical to lay the book out in this way because the collector will almost certainly start, as I did, with humble modern pieces. As he learns more about his subject he will have a solid base from which to reach the earlier dates and will cover the whole field in a way which is unlikely if he starts in the middle or at the far end. Like the archaeologist in his "dig" he has to sift through the more recent layers to reach and understand the older ones. The last hundred years of the pocket watch provide him with an apprenticeship which is all the more important because it is from this field that most of the watches available today will emerge. He will find it difficult and expensive to break through into the antique period.

There is no clear written definition of what constitutes antiquity in a watch or even any oral agreement among dealers. Loosely speaking, and for the purpose of v.a.t., any article over a hundred years old is antique, so the crucial date alters each year. In horology, however, this is probably not correct. The best guidance is probably that given by Clutton and Daniels in *Watches* (1965). Without defining antique, they regard watches dated after 1830 as being modern —the demarcation we should best work to. It also links with the fact that most horological literature finishes here. It is a remarkable coincidence that 1830 should have been chosen as the mystic date. For it was just at this time that the most important single development of the watch took place in this country. This was the general adoption, starting in Lancashire, of the detached lever escapement. Nearly all the recorded horological story is that of the search for such an escapement with negligible frictional rest. It could be thought of as the Old Testament with the fully detached lever in the role of a true or false Messiah. We know now, of course, that this design was indeed the final step in the long search but unfortunately no-one has written a New Testament to record its sweeping and long-lasting success. It would be very unfortunate if the collector was persuaded by the texts to believe that nothing of any importance happened after 1830; it is simply that the romance of the quest for the ideal was over.

My own collection, both in cased watches and uncased movements, is large and varied enough to carry this book back to about 1700 without use of outside material for illustration. The picture of the usual and commonplace watch of the day is best presented by the commonest survivals. It is distorted by reference to unique, exotic or complicated pieces which would naturally be rare both now and in the past. Though a fine watch is very much a thing of beauty, the collector (as opposed to the investor) will get more satisfaction from the five or six ordinary pieces that his money would otherwise buy. Finally, since my watches turned up in a collecting field centred on Liverpool, there is naturally a numerical bias towards the Lancashire watch trade. It is no matter of local loyalty to assert that the part of the Prescot workshops in gaining and keeping the reputation of the English watch has been very much underplayed. During the eighteenth and nineteenth centuries it is probable that most of the movements supplied to watchmakers in this country came from the Lancashire trade. Both the movement and the men who made it were anonymous and the credit went to the finisher who finally engraved the plate.

By 1889 the Prescot trade had so declined that the remaining watchmakers had no alternative but to join the Lancashire Watch Company's factory being built in Prescot. When that failed those who remained had to relapse into the repairing and retailing trade. They were frustrated and embittered craftsmen who saw their skills stamped out by the "shoddy" factory watches. Quite a few became employed by Russells of Liverpool whose workshops were ironically enough mainly casing and repairing the Swiss and Waltham watches which had disrated them. It so happened that my two watchmaker friends, Mr. Stanley Smith and Mr. Robert Phillips, were also employed by Russells at this time. They were able to paint for me the personal effect that the factory watch had had on the decline of the "hand made" watch.

2
The Swiss Watch

UNDER this heading it is not my intention to launch into any detailed story of Swiss chronometry, which is a very long tale indeed. However, in the choice of my title of "The Englishman's Watch" the policy was to cover all watches used in this country which must include those he imported. Such imports will, of course, have survived to be collected and the collector or "watch buff" will need some notes about them. It should be said at once that judging from my own findings, despite the strength of the Swiss industry and its success in exporting to all parts of the world, the real tide of Swiss pocket watches to this country appeared to have set in about 1900. There are two exceptions to this statement—the Geneva "bar" movements and the Roskopf movement. These were, however, cheap watches with a limited life and, like the American Ingersol and the Waterbury, few are to be found in this country today. When found the Geneva is easily recognized by the separate bars or bridges holding the train in place instead of the usual plates. Mostly they were in ladies' watches and always with a cylinder escapement. The Roskopf was a simple pin pallet escapement. Since they only turn up in a worn-out condition and are quite irreparable, few have found their way into my collection. In the twentieth century the Swiss pocket watch could be said to have shared almost the whole of the British market with the Americans (see illustrations Nos. 1–4). In the wrist watch era the Swiss, until very recent years, have captured the whole market.

The comprehensive Bible of Swiss watches is the *Technique and History of the Swiss Watch* by Eugene Jacquet and Alfred Chapuis. The first author "met with untimely death" while Chapuis has written the majority of standard works on many aspects of Swiss watchmaking. The original English translation was made by D. S. Torrens and C. Jenkins and published in 1953. This is out of print but the 1970 reprint takes the story up to 1968 with valuable material on the present-day wrist watch and is still on sale at the astonishingly low price of £3·50. The book is a massive publication of the same size and weight as the standard Clutton and Daniels for English watches and likewise is profusely illustrated, with the emphasis inevitably on the decorative and the complicated. As such, today's collector will find that, as usual, the commonplace pocket watch has been squeezed out. It was simply "the good ordinary watch" and as such of no relative importance. Nevertheless the book is essential to the man who needs the whole background of horology as a basis for this interest.

The setting is what might be expected: "This book will be read like a fine story and we shall be amazed at the wonderful development of the watch industry in Switzerland from the XVIth century to our day". The positive approach grows as one reads on; rarely is there any mention of work in other countries or acknowledgement of their contribution. The negative side fills one with dismay. It explains why we in this country can write objectively about an English trade long dead and buried. We write about our glories in the antique field and our pride in the past. However, we can have little doubt as to why the Swiss left us far behind in the nineteenth century. Both the English and the Swiss trade started in exactly the same way—as a cottage industry—and at roughly the same time. The Swiss progressed quite slowly and carefully to a closely knit industry with training schools and worldwide salesmen. We sat at home as superb individual craftsmen convinced that we made the best watches in the world, secure we thought in our nineteenth century policy of *laisser faire*. As a result our trade was not so much killed by foreign competition; we allowed it to die after cutting its own throat. In comparison with the description of the many Swiss factories which grew up in the nineteenth century, we see only two in our own country. The British Watch Company, inspired by an immigrant Swiss engineer (Ingold), which was smothered at birth, and the Lancashire Watch Company which existed but never flourished between 1889 and 1910. A partial growth on Swiss lines was seen in the small workshops of Coventry (a single exception seems to have been Rotherham & Sons) but these were in comparison petty and unorganized. However, these are futile regrets; let us return to Jaquet and Chapuis.

In Switzerland the industrial development was on different lines from that of America where everything was under one roof: the raw material went in at the back door and the completely finished watch emerged at the front. The Swiss retained their faith in the *ébauche*, the rough movement, or "movement in the grey" of the traditional type—and they still do. They organized the system, however, to the highest efficiency. Originally the *ébauche* was a fairly crude affair, the product of numerous small workshops and needed much further work. It evolved later to the "finissage" (i.e., finishing off) which was ready for the watch factories from which it emerged as the commercial product. Later still, under the aegis of "interchangeability", factories were set up in which all the components were made by machinery. These were supplied to the firms who built the *ébauches*. They were then taken in hand by the companies who finished, rated, cased, decorated and finally exported them under well-known names. In general no one firm made the watch from start to finish though there may have been some exceptions. On the whole only a limited number of types of *ébauche* were used and the whole system was efficient, economic and capable of the highest standards of watchmaking. We read of numerous successes, not only in local observatories but also at Kew and in Washington as well as at International Exhibitions.

With one exception, I have come across only twentieth-century Swiss watches in this country. Many earlier examples will be available to those who search Continental countries and, of course, the odd watch will have been brought in by the traveller. Due to early enthusiasm my own collection shows no less than 61 cased watches and numerous uncased movements. A good number of these resulted from what was looked back on as "the Preston haul". Having finally tracked down an elusive dealer there, he confronted me one Sunday morning with a large brass preserving-pan full to the brim with Swiss movements in rolled gold cases. These were for export to America and he was quite happy for me to take any or all at £2 apiece. His patience was, however, exhausted by the time the twenty best movements had been picked out. In the whole of my group the majority were bought in rolled gold cases and very few in silver. There were a few in Dennison 9ct. cases and one or two in Swiss 14K cases. The only 18ct. cased watch was cased by Benson of London (London, 1930) and named "The Field". It was possible to date only 36 cased watches by means of the hallmark or the Dennison case number. The earliest was 1907, the majority fell between 1916 and 1930, with three odd ones in 1937 and 1938. So we see that the Swiss exports entered the country in bulk fifteen to twenty years later than the American Waltham. By 1925 the Waltham had slumped under the Swiss attack while by 1930 the pocket watch ceased to come in even from Switzerland and the wrist watch took over. The pocket watch continued to be used by those who were loyal to it but it was usually put away in the drawer for the collector of the future to find.

With the English-made watch almost entirely out of the running in the present century, Switzerland and America simply divided the British market between themselves on a basis of mutual competition. A man buying a watch is prepared to pay a good price for something that will last for years with the minimum of repair (as distinct from cleaning). The American Waltham Watch Company concentrated its effort to meet this standard with the "Traveller", an inexpensive but reliable model with minimal jewelling, and they sold millions of them. It could not, however, be expected that the unjewelled holes would last for ever and the public decided it preferred the quality of Swiss watches, with the result that American competition disappeared. Admittedly the extent of jewelling is only one of the criteria of the care and standard that has been put into a watch but usually it is a reliable index; as such it is always stamped on the top plate. The Swiss did indeed make low-jewelled movements and exported them to this country, but the reputation they made for reliability was based on their fully jewelled movements, i.e., fifteen or better. No doubt from choice, only one seven-jewelled movement has found its way into my collection. There were three instances of ten-jewelled movements, all imported, cased and sold by the same firm. This strange number was arrived at by jewelling the additional three holes on the top plate where they could be seen, and omitting this in the bottom plate—a typical deception to improve the appearance though not the quality.

Swiss manufacturers were somewhat coy in naming their movements, so that the top plate will often only carry the stamp "Swiss" or "Swiss made". Of 61 cased watches only 35 carried names of the makers, the other 26 were superficially anonymous. The watch repairer would, however, find the maker of the *ébauche* named or coded inside. A highly organized system was established whereby replacements could be obtained by quoting the number and this still operates for today's wrist watches. In de Carle's *Watch and Clock Encyclopedia* can be found the basic Swiss catalogue number for every watch part and this is extended further to individual makers.

It would not be possible to list all the names that can be found on Swiss pocket watches; they are legion. Jaquet and Chapuis carry an index of watchmakers and other craftsmen up to 1900. Those that occur in my own pocket watches are as follows:

Craftsmen, Criterion, Cyma, Everite, Irani, Limit, Omega, Paul Ditisheim, Peel lever, Peerless, Premier, Presco/Syren, Record, Recta, Revue, Roamer, Rolex, Transpacific, Trojan, Unicorn, Vertex, and Zenith.

These are clearly only a few of the many who were making watches in this narrow span of the exporting years of the pocket watch to this country. If one included the wrist watches an analysis of only the named makers would need a book in itself. As to casing, relatively few entered the country in Swiss cases of gold or rolled gold, but some American rolled gold cases turned up. The majority apparently entered the country as movements and were cased by the Dennison Watch Case Company of Birmingham and stamped A.L.D.

A limited number of pocket watches are still made in Switzerland and continue to reach this country. They follow on from the dress watch (see later), being of the same size but even slimmer and more streamlined. As such they are carried in the breast pocket and anchored with a chain and gilt button in the buttonhole of the lapel. A more robust pocket watch is also made for the use of people such as bus drivers and engine drivers. This is the successor to the railway watch which in the heyday of the railways in this country was issued to employees. Electricians sometimes favour such a watch, as even the anti-magnetic wrist watch sometimes succumbs when used in certain magnetic fields. The only other section that remains loyal to the pocket watch and chain today is the legal profession, and recently one of my watches (a Swiss movement) graced the person of a young barrister pleading his first cause. A waistcoat is, however, essential with a watch and chain, and recently young people, who of course have no recollection of the pocket watch in everyday use, are looking for one as a gimmick. They eschew the open face and insist on a hunter or half-hunter case.

It remains to describe the only nineteenth-century Swiss watch that has come my way, no doubt having been brought to this country by a tourist or traveller. It is a very elegant watch with an intriguingly designed movement. There is no means of dating it, but it is thought to be between 1860 and 1870. The dial is large with slim tall numerals and a centre sweep hand; the watch itself is also slim and cased in unstamped silver. The bow is D-shaped and a push-piece opens the back. The movement has an inner sprung glass dome pierced for winding and setting by key. Intricate decoration and engraving has been used throughout and there is no top plate. Instead it has skeletonization and individualized bridges with one most unusual exception. The barrel pivots only on the bottom plate. It is jewelled to seventeen jewels, the escapement is a detached lever with a decorated tail. The scope of the balance wheel is enlarged by the attachment to the rim of four battle-axe-shaped steel forms. After overhaul by Mr. R. E. Phillips it rates perfectly, but it should be noted that Mr. Phillips pursed his lips over the standard of mechanical design. It demonstrates perfectly the versatility and style that the Swiss watchmakers could reach. Its provenance baffled everybody since there was no maker's name and the only clue was an ideograph engraved on the back and repeated on the movement. As far as could be ascertained this was in some obscure oriental language or more likely a concocted trademark on the lines of a "doodle". Jaquet and Chapuis provided the answer with a page of illustrations of such watches. It was made specially for the Chinese market. An identical watch was made by the Bovets of Fleurier who were called the "Bovets of China". In fact these watches became known as "Bovets".

France was concentrating on her clocks and it is probably true to say that in watches she was running down from the great days of Breguet. I have come across no examples from Holland or Germany, and none of the other Continental countries appears to be in the running. America was at the beginning of her great factory era with a policy of watches for the masses with a prototype of the very ordinary watch. This country was turning out the utilitarian watch to a standard pattern, albeit of very good workmanship, and understandably little was written about them. We can only look to an American, Paul M. Chamberlain in his book *It's About Time*, to give us an international viewpoint, on which my summary is based. The English texts have very little indeed to say about the Swiss watch or the Swiss trade, possibly because so few examples reached this country. Clutton and Daniels, however, in their book *Watches* have the following significant but almost "throw away" comment: "It was in Switzerland, towards the end of Breguet's life (1823), that the stage was being set for the mass produced watch, which was eventually to give supremacy in horology to Switzerland and, finally, produce watches whose accuracy would even surpass the finest work of Breguet and Arnold". Significant though this statement is it was not subsequently taken up or enlarged upon. What the "bovet" shows then is not only the almost casual expertise of the Swiss watchmaker but it finally justifies the whole tone which carries through Jaquet and Chapuis. It certainly is a "fine story" both of technical skill and closely reasoned trade organization. It is certainly something to bear very much in mind when we blow our insular trumpet over the past glories of the English watch.

3

The Waltham Pocket Watch

THE scope of this book aims to cover almost all those watches likely to be found by the modest collector. This includes those made in this country and those which were imported. Of those imported the greatest number from a single maker were those of the American Waltham Watch Company. They were so common that my collection includes 63 cased watches, many uncased movements, and a few early movements. All the complete watches have been put back into working order which is not only a credit to my watch repairs but also to the reliability and interchangeability of the movements. The Elgin Watch Company and the Hamilton Watch Company also exported watches to this country but they would both appear to have been much less popular as they are represented in the collection by only a few from each firm—far too few for me to make any representations about them. All three makers were quite large businesses but it looks as if Waltham had the more active export policy and the better salesmen. It should, however, be noted that they had an extremely good product to sell and because of their slick factory organization they could sell it at the right price. This is the other side of the coin to the English watchmakers, whose few attempts at a factory-made watch failed and whose hand-made or hand-finished watches were priced out of the reach of millions who wanted to buy a watch. At the present time many families still treasure Grandfather's watch as a family heirloom. The odds are 10 to 1 that when you come to examine the watch it will be a Waltham movement. (Great-grandfather's watch would be an English lever.) We are now thinking about the reservoir of watches still in existence. It is still quite large for sentimental reasons but every so often (for unsentimental reasons) the family watch or watches are sold and the collector has his opportunity.

The American Waltham Watch Company only survived to reach great success after a long struggle. This is described in the booklet *The History of the A.W.W.Co. of Waltham, Mass.*, by Henry G. Abbott. This was originally published as one of a series of articles in *The American Jeweller* and reprinted separately in 1905. The author points out that America had nothing to do with the important rudimentary inventions which accounted for the basic development of the watch. But "while the makers of Europe were having their trains made by one man or family, their balances by another, their assembling done in one house and their adjusting done in another, we have been erecting factories in which the watch was manufactured complete and ready to be placed upon the market, a monument to American genius". Indeed it was, but the Swiss were doing the same thing and going through the same torments, though with more lasting success. At the beginning of the nineteenth century watches in America were hand-made, largely from materials imported from Europe. Before this, fully finished watches were imported and a great deal of this trade was from Lancashire, travelling via Liverpool. The first factory attempts to produce American verges, in 1809 and 1812, failed because of competition from Switzerland. Nothing further was attempted until 1849 when A. L. Dennison interested Edward Howard, a manufacturing watchmaker, in the possibility of trying again and obtained backing from a Mr. Curtis. The first watch was produced in 1850. For the next 10 years things were very precarious and the ownership, the name and the location changed several times, until it settled in 1855 in Waltham, Mass., and took the name of the American Watch Company. A first dividend was declared in 1860 but next year the Civil War broke out and there was an all-round slump. Later, however, the war, as is always the case, increased the demand for watches and enabled the company to get on its feet and stay there. In 1861 Dennison, who had been superintendent of the factory, finally lost heart and resigned. This was ironic because after the next year the company never looked back. Dennison, after several further unsuccessful attempts both in America and Switzerland, finally found the prosperity he sought making watch cases in England. As a reversal of this, some at least of the Waltham success was due to Lancashire tradesmen who were tempted to leave the cottage industry of watchmaking in this country and enter the factory life in Massachusetts. They were men out of character, for the majority opted to stay with the old methods until the present industry was dying on its feet. The majority of the survivors among the craftsmen was persuaded—indeed they had little option—to enter the factory of the Lancashire Watch Company of Prescot when it was set up in 1889. This they did with little enthusiasm and they gave up their old-fashioned workbenches with great reluctance.

It seems unlikely that the industrialization of the watch industry could have succeeded in this country against the inertia of centuries of traditional methods. Both Dennison and Howard saw prophetically that the world was ready for mass production and believed, contrary to the traditional view, that this could be done in the case of the watch. They believed watch parts could be standardized to such a degree of fine accuracy that they could be interchangeable, thus making both manufacture and repair very much easier. They believed too that all the processes could be streamlined to flow evenly under one roof so that every specialist's output would be at a maximum. Even more daring, they believed many of the processes could be automated and that machines could be designed to produce all the parts needed and do some if not all the assembly. These were visionary claims but eventually they all proved possible at Waltham and in other countries—with, of course, the exception of our own. It is interesting that originally, from 1865 to 1890, Waltham produced its own watch cases. The silver were made in the Waltham factory and the gold were made in New York. In 1890 there were sufficient case-making factories for the American Waltham Watch Company to drop this side of their work and produce only the finished movements.

The number of movements produced by the factory is both fantastic and fascinating. The early figures are given in the history of the company as follows: for the first thirty years up to 1884 about two and a half million. By 1894 this had grown to nearly six million and by 1904 the total stood at twelve million. It was also asserted that there were no blank runs in the numerical sequence: unfortunately watchmakers have always been eclectic in their choice of numbers and, for instance, could well number their first watch at 1,000 and count from there. Luckily totals given above join nicely into a skeleton table I have constructed from the case dates of my own watches. True, this is patchy and spread thin over the years, but on the whole it is quite symmetrical. There are a few anomalies but these can be ignored without weakening the table. They may be due to recasing or to the holding in stock of movements supplied from the factory in previous years. As we know, the factory only made uncased movements after 1890 and these came into this country, wrapped in waterproof paper, in neat flat tins. There may have been a lower duty when importing uncased movements (and indeed possibly empty cases) than on complete watches. However, the majority of Waltham movements reaching this country were cased in Dennison Watch Case Company's cases after import. So by reading the hallmark or finding the year code on the rolled gold case it was possible to arrive at a useful correlation between serial number and date of manufacture in the forty-six of my watches. Because it is bound to be only a fair approximation there is no point in dealing with individual numbers. But even using the nearest million can be of great help to the collector who wishes (as he should) to date his movements. The anomalous numbers have been set in italics in the table rather than omitted.

AMERICAN WALTHAM WATCH COMPANY

Approximate Correlation of Serial Numbers and Date of Manufacture

Date	Number (in millions)		Date	Number (in millions)	
1884	2,515,119	(Actual)	1911	15,16,12,15,16M	(Actual)
1885	2M	(Estimated)	1912	16M	(Estimated)
1886	2M	(,,)	1913	16M	(,,)
1887	2M	(,,)	1914	17,18,17,18M	(Actual)
1888	3M	(,,)	1915	———	
1889	3M	(,,)	1916	19,25,19M	(,,)
1890	3M	(,,)	1917	20,20M	(,,)
1891	4M	(,,)	1918	22M	(,,)
1892	4M	(,,)	1919	22M	(,,)
1893	5M	(,,)	1920	22,21,22,22,22M	(,,)
1894	5,897,035	(Actual)	1921	22M	(,,)
1895	6M	(Estimated)	1922	22M	(,,)
1896	6M	(,,)	1923	22,23,22,23M	(,,)
1897	7M	(,,)	1924	———	
1898	7M	(,,)	1925	23,22,23,23M	(,,)
1899	8M	(,,)	1926	22M	(,,)
1900	8M	(,,)	1927	24M	(Estimated)
1901	9M	(,,)	1928	25M	(,,)
1902	10M	(,,)	1929	25M	(,,)
1903	11M	(,,)	1930	26M	(,,)
1904	12,000,000	(Actual)	1931	*29M*	(Actual)
1905	12M,11M,12M	(,,)	1932	27M	(Estimated)
1906	10M,11M	(,,)	1933	27M	(Actual)
1907	———		1934	28M	(Estimated)
1908	———		1935	28M	(,,)
1908	15M,14M	(,,)	1936	29M	(,,)
1909	15M,15M,	(,,)	1937	29M	(,,)
1910	———		1938	30M	(,,)
			1939	31M	(Actual)
			1940	31M,29M	(,,)

N.B. Own figures from 1905 onwards.

From this table we can arrive at an approximate average output each year on the following lines:

1884 to 1894	·33 million per annum		1915 to 1924	·50 million per annum
1895 to 1904	·62 million per annum		1925 to 1934	·30 million per annum
1905 to 1914	·60 million per annum		1935 to 1940	·60 million per annum

The first five lines of this output table fit in very much with what we would expect, but it is difficult to understand the rise in production over the late thirties when the company, as I understand it, was failing. The maximum daily output of the factory was stated to be up to 3,500 movements per day in 1944. Depending on how many working days there were in the year, say about 280, this would have given about a million movements per annum. From the estimated figures this total might well have been attained in the early nineteen-hundreds but it almost certainly fell off later.

Since setting up my own table of serial numerbs based on survivals which have found their way into my collection I have come across what purports to be the official list—though there is no information where this was published. This is headed "Approximate production date of Waltham serial numbers". The years are irregularly spaced and the numbers of movements produced is given in round millions. The table runs from 1857 (1,000 movements) to 1948 when a total of 33,000,000 movements had been produced. The two tables agree fairly well but the official numbers of movements made by any one year are consistently ahead of my deduced figures. This lag can reasonably be accounted for by the time taken for a movement to leave the factory stores, be exported and distributed in this country, and finally be cased by the retailer to be sold over the counter. Providing the serial numbers ran continuously without any blanks then the official figures show that the output in the 1890s was half a million a year. From 1901 to 1908 the output was a million a year. Thereafter the output fluctuated at about half a million a year with the exception of the later years of World War I when production again rose to one million.

I have not found any Waltham pocket watches with a higher serial number than 31 million in this country nor any evidence that any were imported after 1939—any, that is, that were on sale to the public. Nor did any appear to come in 1945. They were, however, extensively used as a Government Issue by American troops in this country and army repair shops were well supplied with full kits of repair parts. Some of these watches may have stayed in this country. Our own Government was, as might be expected, desperately short of issue watches, particularly at the beginning of World War II, and there was only perhaps one factory (Smiths) to meet the demand. In the main our supply was from Switzerland and the movements, often of very high quality, were cased here in gunmetal cases. It is possible that some movements may have come from America.

Early Waltham movements are obviously more likely to be found in America; but there are two in my collection which must be very early by English standards. Both are Crescent Garden movements by the A. W. Co. of Waltham, Mass. The first is in a silver case by A.W.Co. and is still keeping good time after overhaul and being given new hands. It is a "going barrel", key wind, three-quarter plate nine-jewel, plain gold balance pattern, with winding and setting on the top plate. The number is 819,940 so that it can only be dated roughly as between 1877, when the first million movements were completed, and 1885, when the title of A.W.Co. was changed to the American Waltham Watch Co. However, on the back of the bottom plate is engraved (not stamped) the date Feb 14, 1865, indicating presumably that this batch of bottom plates was made on that day. Regulation was by a modern index on a plain modern cock and there was a patent pinion (not yet a safety pinion). The second Crescent Garden movement was uncased and has a broken balance staff. It differs from the other movement in having a modern cut bimetallic balance with timing screws which presumably is original. The number is 819,655, i.e., slightly earlier than the first movement. The bottom plate, however, is identically engraved Feb. 14, 1865. One can only guess at the significance of both the dating of the bottom plate itself (surely a very unusual practice in watchmaking) and then the use of the same dated batch of plates for a run of individual movements.

The complete Waltham story must be written from America but there can be no doubt that though their exporting activities—given this immense output—must have been world-wide, a very great impact was made upon the English watch industry. It was in fact a fatal impact, which only a few had foreseen and fewer still had had the courage to point out. The theme song might have been "There'll always be an English Lever", but by the end of the nineteenth century there were very few, either at home or abroad, who could afford this carriage-trade standard. Everybody wanted a watch and the irony was that these "shoddy" machine-made watches from Switzerland and America could be reliable as well as cheap. Ignoring the cheap Ingersol and Waterbury, and outrunning the Elgin and the Hamilton, Waltham captured almost the complete demand for pocket watches in this country as far as America was concerned. They divided it with the Swiss market, but my collection suggests that Waltham were in earlier than the Swiss and sold more watches. However, this was not the whole story and just as the English watch trade failed for lack of foresight so was Waltham overtaken by events.

Soon after 1900 it began to be fashionable, in this country at least, for ladies to wear their watches on the wrist—it was certainly more convenient than on a chain or brooch. Initially the A.W.W.Co. had always made a lady's watch, size 10, which was suitable for this treatment. During World War I the British Army suddenly found this feminine fashion to be just the thing for active service. (Again it should be noted how wars always stimulate changes in horology.) There were, of course, no specifically made or designed wrist watches and all kinds were pressed into use and in general must have proved much inferior to a pocket watch. However, the wrist watch, for some years after this, was regarded as an effeminate European fashion as far as American men were concerned and they continued with their pocket watches until resistance suddenly crumbled. This delay allowed the Swiss to push ahead with research and design and gain many years' start over Waltham. Though basically the wrist watch is on the same principle as the pocket watch, widespread changes and improvements are needed before the wrist watch can match the pocket watch for reliability. There was more to it than strapping a pocket watch on the wrist, which was more or less what Waltham did. As a result the public soon learned that Swiss wrist watches were very much superior and needed far less attention. In the 1930s the A.W.W.Co. was in a decline and though apparently respited by Government work in 1940 they did not survive the return of peace to send any more watches to this country. The name of Waltham is now, I am told, being used by a Swiss company.

At first the lady's size 10 watch was used but it did not stand up to wrist wear for several reasons. A wrist watch has to be designed to take sudden movements, direct knocks, increased liability to becoming magnetized, awkward use of the sleeve, and increased exposure to damp and dirt. The sleeve mechanism in the size 10 watch was not robust enough; it broke or even perished, and often had to be repaired. The single roller escapement would jam with sudden movement and was later replaced by a double roller. Those pivots that were un-jewelled wore quickly under wrist watch conditions and owing to their smallness, compared with the pocket watch, gave a much shorter life. It was Mr. Stanley Smith's practice, using quick "pop-in" jewels to make the 7-jewel movement fully jewelled with very good results. This implied, of course, that the basic best seller in the Waltham range was really a non-starter as a long-life wrist watch. On the other hand, the Swiss had early learnt the need for full jewelling, with the result that they earned a reputation for reliability that was much higher than the Waltham. The A.W.W. Company indeed made efforts to cope with these defects in their wrist watches and sought Swiss advice, but they did not really design a wrist watch *de novo* and so fell too far back in the race to recover.

Of this enormous flood of pocket watches one cannot tell how many reached this country or accurately when they began to come in, but from my examples it would seem that 1905 marked the beginning of large numbers. It may be that import regulations favoured the American watch after that date and influenced the numbers at other times. I am told that Waltham watches were well known in this country before 1905, some under the older names which are usually only to be found in America; but this early field has not been a fruitful one for me. The prototype of the first watch was made by Dennison in 1850.

Subsequently the thread of the original company ran through different titles and in 1859 took the name of the American Watch Company. In 1885 it assumed the full title of the American Waltham Watch Company. Among my older movements there are five engraved for the American Watch Company which presumably should date before 1885. Of these four have numbers between one and two million, while the fifth has a seven-million number. These older movements are mostly full plate with the cock and balance mounted on the top plate. Two early movements, both smaller and with hunter three o'clock winds, are three-quarter plate. All are regulated with the modern index on the cock, many years ahead of this mode in England. All have "going barrels" (without dummy barrels) at a time when fusees were invariably used in this country.

Giving particular watches in a company's range individual and no doubt registered names, was in my experience unusual before 1900. The Swiss limited themselves to "Swiss Made, 15 jewels", the actual name of the firm being hidden away. To a certain extent the Waltham company followed this, giving only the company name and the number of jewels—a 15-jewelled watch told the buyer it was fully jewelled. However, from early days the A.W.W. Company favoured names, which of course was helpful in advertising. The older names are matters for the American collector and of the few that reached this country those post-1905 in my hands show all the important groups.

The hierarchy of Waltham elegance and excellence in movements runs on the following scale:

The 7-Jewel Movement. This was given several names of which the Traveller has predominated in this country (also Beacon and Bond Street). It was the cheapest and most popular watch against which the methods and prices of the Lancashire Watch Company were unable to compete in the early days of this century. Jewels were given to the roller, the balance (endcapped), and pallets. The pallet staff, the escape wheel, the fourth wheel, the third wheel and the centre wheel were unjewelled. Though the watch was reliable, eventually the pivot holes in the plates wore oval. They could, of course, be re-bushed if the rest of the watch justified this expense. As can be seen in the illustrations, the design was completely modern with a compensated balance. The earlier movements were gilded and the later polished nickel. Some of the movements arrived in this country cased, for instance, by the Illinois Case Co., but the majority were cased here by Dennison Cases. Probably, by virtue of complete interchangeability, the retailer bought both separately and sometimes added his name to the backplate while his "watchmaker" made the final assembly. One would have expected that with such an inexpensive item the case would have been invariably one of rolled gold or occasionally silver, but quite a few of the movements were thought by the customer to be worth at least a 9-carat case, another tribute to Waltham reliability.

The 9-Jewel Movement. This was sometimes given the series name of Premier. It was an out-of-line development since it would have been much more suitable to make an 11-jewel model to bridge the gap between the 7- and the 15-jewel. The additional pair was awarded to the 'scape wheel pivots. It seems to have been rarely made, and only two examples are noted in my collection. One was distinguished as a "swing ring" casing, a throw-back to previous centuries where the movement was hinged to the case and swung out for inspection. In this instance there is, as was essential, a tight-fitting screw-cap dust cover. The other example of this design is an uncased 15-jewel movement.

The 15-Jewel Movement. We are now on more reliable and long-wearing ground with all the pivots except the centre wheel and barrel being jewelled. The group of about thirty watches and movements in the collection suggests a large output. At one end of the scale of development we see the early introduction of the three-quarter plate. This is a size 16 movement made by the American Watch Company with a serial number of 1·7 million, both points that would date it about 1880. This is oddly enough a 13-jewel movement, the third wheel being unjewelled; the name given to it is the Hillside. Another identical movement is a little earlier (1·1 million) and is unnamed. At the other end of the scale full plate movements with the balance wheel on the back plate were still being made in 15-jewelling to a much later date. One with a serial number of 11 million would be on my scale about 1906. Another, in the 18 million range would be about 1914 and a third—20 million—would be about 1917 and has a 1917 hallmark on the case. These made bulky watches of unfashionable size for those days. The silver case in one instance is stamped $2\frac{1}{2}$ oz. and none of these three movements is given any name. Names were in fact thinly scattered and most of these movements travelled simply on the heading of 15-jewel Walthams. The title Duke appears on one. Another almost masquerades by being named Traveller, a symbol which seems exclusively reserved for the Waltham 7 but perhaps the extra jewelling had been done later by some skilful watchmaker. The third movement, which is of good quality, has the name of Riverside. It is numbered 4·7 million, i.e., about 1890, and has a cam regulator which is noted by Chamberlain to have been used by Waltham but of which I have no other example. Presumably some time after 1890 the Riverside movement was redesigned on the more usual 19-jewel lines. On the subject of regulators nearly all the 15-jewel movements are fitted with a more sophisticated type than the straight index finger. This was usually the star wheel type seen in the illustrations. Chamberlain notes it as a multiplying leverage system on the basis of Mershon's patent of 1859. This was used by Edward Howard, Dennison's first partner, and subsequently on the Waltham watch. On the higher grade watches the side screw type was used. This was also used by Edward Howard for his watches, under a patent granted to Geo. P. Reed in 1865. The highly descriptive name given to this regulator was that of "the whiplash".

The 17-Jewel Waltham. We are now entering the high-class field with good finish and long life. This group of sixteen watches seem fairly equally divided into the anonymous, the Royal, and the P. S. Bartlett. Superficially they all seem similar, with the centre wheel now jewelled, and most have micrometer regulators. They are all very fine watches but it would not be surprising to find that the customer paid more for a Royal than for the ordinary movement and much more for the P. S. Bartlett. However, more care was given to inspection and rating, for both the named movements carry the word "adjusted" on the back plate. We would expect the choice of the name Royal to be a compliment to Mr. Royal E. Robbins who joined the original company in 1858 and remained its Treasurer for forty-five years. He was succeeded in the post by his son—also named Royal. History relates that the much-sought-after P.S.B. was specifically named after Pattern Sergeant Bartlett who at the age of twenty-one started work in the newly opened factory at Waltham in 1855. He quickly became head of the screw and plate department. In 1859 the American Watch Company put on the market a new 18-size movement on which they engraved P. S. Bartlett and they repeated this honour two years later when they made a size 10 lady's watch. Not long afterwards, however, Bartlett was induced to become one of the highly paid team to start the Elgin Watch Company, Waltham's most serious American competitor. He did subsequently return to Waltham for a while but finally set up his own business—albeit in Elgin. It might therefore be presumed that P. S. Bartlett watches may have been in production for most of the company's life though possibly not in the later stages, for my examples appear only between the years 1909 and 1920.

The 19-Jewel Movement. Only one name seems to have been used here—the Riverside. This is not a surprising choice, for the whole length of the Waltham factory backs on to the River Charles. These are prestige watches and it is likely that not many were made. They are difficult to find but I have three examples. One is dated 1911, and two 1914. The symbols of class vary from watch to watch. They are engraved as being adjusted in five positions. The centre wheel gives the impression of being gold and contrasts with the other brass parts. Sometimes the balance wheel timing screws look like gold in a bimetallic balance. The head of the pallet cock and the raised jewel holders in the back plate seem golden too. It is refreshing to see that the escape wheel is still of steel and third and fourth wheels are still brazen. The wind is fascinating in its smoothness. Such a watch holds its own with anything produced in America, Switzerland or this country.

It will be seen that I have used the word gold with some caution and this is justified. At first sight gold would not seem suitable for train wheels in view of its softness, but this can be overcome by using a suitable alloy and varying the proportion of gold. In the Riverside Maximus it is generally agreed that what appears to be golden is in fact gold. In the lesser, though still high-grade, breeds of Waltham what appears to be gold may either be real or gold plated. Superficially, of course the difference cannot be detected.

The 21-Jewel Movement. This is rare. I had recently the good fortune to run a 21-jewel movement to earth and uncover the reason for its elusiveness. It proved to be a centre sweep seconds watch made during the Second World War for the American government as a G.I. instrument. It appeared in a war surplus catalogue was available in this country post-war, and any that turn up now will have come from this source. It is worth noting in passing that both Elgin and Hamilton made a 21-jewel movement and there are two of each of these in my collection. One of the Hamiltons is in screw-back rolled gold case from the Illinois Case Company of Elgin. It is engraved, of course, Hamilton Watch Company, Lancaster, Pa., and carries the word "adjusted". It is on very much the same lines as the 23-jewel Waltham with what appears to be gold wheels, timing studs, jewel holders and so on. The Elgin 21-jewel is similarly sophisticated with a similar lavish display of gold. It differs only in having the escape wheel, the fourth wheel and the third wheel mounted on separate cocks in the continental style. It has been suggested that both Hamilton and Elgin felt the additional pair of extra jewels added nothing to the efficiency of the watch and rested their competition at twenty-one. It is important to note that all three leading American companies made a watch of the highest possible standard. These watches were all similar and all traditional. They stood at the high-water mark of the development of the pocket watch—any further advances were to be made within the framework of the wrist watch.

The 23-Jewel Movement. This is the ultimate in jewelling of the pocket watch, though wrist watches have managed to raise the number even higher by means of further endcapping. It looks as if the escape wheel and pallet staff pivots have been endcapped here. In addition the barrel arbour is either jewelled or in some instances is surrounded or replaced by a ruby staff. They appear under two names, the later being that of Vanguard. My three Vanguards puzzle me as they vary so much in standard and style. The oldest—serial number 25 million, i.e., the late 1920s—just about reaches the finish of the Riverside. It is credited with adjustment in six positions and a Lossier inner terminal hairspring though both third and fourth wheels are of brass. The wind is exceptionally smooth. The two younger movements—both in the 29 million range, i.e., the late 1930s—have a relatively crude finish with an odd mixture of gold and brass parts. The latest, though the gold centre wheel is still present, is down to utility standards otherwise. The same plain undecorated utility standard is also shown by a 9-jewel movement which, with a number in the 31 million range, must have been among the last Waltham watches to enter the country. The impression left with me is that of the Waltham Company falling away from its previous high standards as it struggled to survive, against the competition of the wrist watch.

On the other hand, the 23 jewel-Riverside Maximus is a name to conjure with. These are rare birds but there is a mixed bag of four in my collection. They date back to the palmy days of sweet success and were no doubt given the most careful grooming. In a heavy gold hunter case they were indeed the prestige presentation watch, fit for a President. I first learnt of this rare jewel from an old and disillusioned watchmaker in Blackpool. He felt that the place had sadly declined from the days when his customers who really had "the brass" proved it by owning a Maximus. It was only a few weeks after this that I made my first buy in Chester. The manager of the shop in which it lay was disinclined to sell. Not because he knew it for what it was but because he lent it out to his customers whose watches were under repair. To deter me he priced it at an absurd price (from his point of view) considering it had but a very worn rolled gold case. There were false values on both sides of the counter when he was paid what was asked; but such are the triumphs of the collector. It is worth saying a few words about each of these four watches.

The first is a lady's watch, full hunter, size 10. Unfortunately it is not complete, lacking a bezel which is impossible to replace. The case is 10K gold (U.S. assay) and unlike so many similar lady's watchcases it is in full repair. Strangely, the movement is only 19-jewel though clearly marked Riverside Maximus. The embellishments are of gold to the full standard. The serial number of 10 million suggests a date of about 1905.

The second is a decorated dress watch in white gold case made by the Elgin Giant Watch Case Company to 14K standard. Both the back and the front of the case open from one hinge and there is no dome. The serial number is 23 million, giving it a date in the early twenties. The gold standard is incomplete as the third and fourth wheels are clearly brass. After overhaul it is in perfect working order.

The third piece is the normal-size pocket watch mentioned above. Everything is to the highest standard with the back plate broken up into a bridge for the centre, third and fourth wheels and a separate cock for the 'scape wheel. This displays the gold wheels, I am told that the jewelling is by means of real matched rubies and sapphires in contrast to the more usual synthetic stones. It is lettered "adjusted" but no mention is made of any positions. The regulator is the usual micrometer type and the watch is in full running order after overhaul. The serial number is 12 million, giving its age as about 1905. The worn rolled gold case has been discreetly discarded for a 9ct. case by Benson Bros. (B.B.) of Liverpool which is more suitable for a movement of this standard.

The fourth movement came to me with a story of it being the pride and joy of an old watchmaker who, of course, knew its standing. He finally sold it in some complicated deal to a retailer-dealer who knew of my interest. His idea was to reverse the usual "gold rush" ploy, rehouse it in a gold case, and make a nice profit. The case was not even rolled gold—it was cupro-nickel and very badly worn at that. Luckily it was possible to persuade the dealer to take his profit from me and let me have the watch as it stood. Like the previous movement it is fully embellished, beautifully finished and on overhaul found to be in wonderful condition. It must be significant that both these superlative movements should have turned up in such rubbishy cases. The lesson to be learnt by the collector is to open every watch met with despite the poorest of cases.

There is unfortunately no example in my collection of Walthams of a railway watch, but this is hardly surprising since there was no reason for them to be exported. The American railway scene, before the advent of the automobile, was a very complex picture with many crossovers and common-usage tracks. Precise timing for arrival at a junction was very important. Drivers were therefore supplied with railway watches of rather large size and in many cases the watches were overhauled and retimed at regular intervals. Most of the watchmaking companies tendered for this type of work and probably Hamilton was credited with the highest standard. However, the A.W.W. Company also supplied railway watches but information as to standards and patterns seems to have been retained in the U.S.A.

If I seem to have devoted overmuch time to an American watch it is simply because it is the watch most likely to come the collector's way today and tomorrow. To my mind the pocket-watch man must know his Walthams backwards. However, the only reference to this very wide field in the English texts is a passing note of high praise from Camerer Cuss for the Riverside Maximus. It should be added here that there seems to be a similar lack of guidance in this country in regard to the large numbers of Swiss pocket watches that were imported. Possibly in America (and in Switzerland) books may well be available to fill the gaps.

Having spent some time in painting the Waltham scene in America it might be helpful to look at the effect of this success on the trade in this country. In the township of Prescot, eight miles from Liverpool, there can still be seen some of the greenhouse-like workshops and the North-facing attic windows where in the nineteenth century a large part of the English lever trade was built. Before setting up his factory Dennison visited Prescot in 1850 to see the English competition of cottage industry organization which had been described by his Lancashire emigrant workers. He found it even worse than he had been told. It confirmed his view that a going barrel lever watch made in a precision factory organization could be a world-beater. So it was, and when others followed his lead Prescot and Coventry were unable to compete.

4

The Rise of the Wristlet Watch

WE must see how and why the pocket watch came to be ousted by the wrist watch over the last fifty years. Since my collection contains nothing other than traditional pocket watches this will be a theoretical exercise, but no doubt in the future collectors will be hunting for wristlets with just as much interest. The idea of using the wrist to carry the watch is by no means new and we are told that in the seventeenth century Queen Elizabeth had a bracelet watch in her collection. Ring watches, small enough to fit the finger, had also been made—John Arnold made an outstanding example in 1764. The Swiss are credited with a more extensive entry into the field from 1850 onwards (Eric Bruton). The use was, however, restricted to ladies' wear in the form of jewellery. Masculine use would appear to have started in the British Army but it has not been possible to find out either the date or the campaign which gave rise to it, but it must have been before 1900 and was no doubt confined to the Regular Army Officer. Volunteers going off to the Boer War (1899 to 1902) modelled themselves on the Regulars by taking with them the fob watches of their wives and sweethearts to wear on the wrist. Since it is well known that a lady's watch "is never in repair" the timekeeping must have been hardly very useful. Since lugs for the strap were unknown in this country at that time the watch was secured in a cup or pocket on the wrist strap. Eric Bruton attributes this primitive strap and cup to E. A. Pearson, a London saddler and dates it as just before World War I.

Traditionally, if and when the volunteers returned from the Boer War they returned the watches to their ladies and went back to the pocket watch again.

While no doubt small-size pocket watches were converted extensively, the Swiss, apparently the only people to see any future in this trend, soon rose to the challenge with purpose-built wrist watches. By about 1910 they were ready to export to this country wrist watches, no doubt miniature pocket watches with proper lugs for a strap, designed to be worn by men. This was uphill work on the sales side for wristlets were by long tradition feminine or in schoolboy terms "cissy".

When World War I came along in 1914 there was again a great demand for a small pocket watch or ladies' watch to which wire lugs were brazed and for which the saddlers made the strap. In some cases metal grilles were used to protect the watch glass.

The military-effect action of that time, which lingered on, was to shoot the cuff in an exaggerated sweep of the arm to read the time on the outer side of the wrist. Wearing the watch on the outer side has persisted since, though it is much more exposed to damage. It has always seemed to me that the inner side of the wrist was a safer and less ostentatious place—the strap being reversed, of course.

During the last years of the war an essential present to every young man going overseas was his first wrist watch. When the young men came home this was then the badge of the ex-soldier and in all European countries from this point the use of the wrist watch spread at the expense of the pocket watch.

America only managed to get a relatively small expeditionary force to France in World War I, but when these soldiers came home they met opposition to the idea of their wrist watches. The idea was still effete and effeminate and remained so well into the 1920s; European visitors were still signalled by their bracelets. The sound man still carried a pocket watch, but the effect of this resistance to change meant that the American watch companies allowed the Swiss to get a ten or even twenty years lead in the design and development of the wristlet. An efficient wrist watch is very much more than a scaled-down pocket watch and the Americans never caught up on the Swiss lead. This is at least the lesson taught by the English market, on which the American wristlet has never made any impression—other than one of a high rate of repair. Even the much later Japanese and Russian designs or copies have done better.

By 1939 and World War II the wristlet watch was, of course, firmly established. Issue watches to the British forces were of both types, the allocation possibly depending on rank and the type of duty to be undertaken. A recently republished picture of Edward VII about 1910, shows the watch in the left-hand breast pocket with the strap or chain going horizontally across to the opposite breast pocket.

Only the high-grade Swiss wristlet stood up to active service in heat, damp, dust, and the activities of native repairers. As always in wars, the first trophy to be taken by the winners from the dead, wounded, or prisoner losers was the watch. In contrast to World War I, Switzerland was now much more cut off from this country and the open markets of the Middle East provided the troops the opportunity to buy their watches.

The detached lever was, and largely remains, the escapement of the wrist watch on the grounds of reliability and cheapness. The self-winding watch has the advantage of keeping the mainspring constantly fully wound. The modern self-winding watch was patented by John Harwood in this country in 1923 but it failed, as usual on financial grounds, and had to wait till the 1950s to be taken up successfully in Switzerland. Quite by chance I recently came across John Harwood's son still in business as a watchmaker in the little village of Dunster near Minehead.

Further advances have been by the way of the electric battery, the tuning fork and the quartz crystal, and Tissot's all-plastic watch advertised as needing no lubrication or maintenance. The present-day peak is the quartz crystal read-out watch, which would seem to have ended the constant horological struggle in that it has no moving parts. These movements, however, are expensive and no doubt the lever will continue for many years yet, since it is perfectly adequate for everyday use. Since repairers will become even fewer in the future, it is likely that when the timing machine shows any significant trouble a new or rebuilt movement will be put in and the old one sent back to the parent factory.

5
The "Going-Barrel" English Lever Watch

As we shall see the fusee and chain method of providing constant torque to the output of the mainspring was necessary because high quality mainsprings could not be made in the earlier days. As the standard of mainsprings improved they reached a stage when a constant torque could be relied upon whatever the winding state of the spring throughout its cycle. It was then possible to take the drive direct from a wheel integral with the barrel which was then termed to be a "going barrel". As Mr. J. B. Polding of Manchester points out in a personal communication: "I do not think that the quality of the mainspring was a significant factor in the continued use of the fusee. The fusee was at first essential with the verge escapement because changes in the torque had a serious effect on the rate. This was also present in the lever escapement to a lesser degree before isochronism was understood. Therefore the English watchmaker's desire for perfection, coupled with his reluctance to change, were probably the main reasons for the retention of the fusee. It was finally finished by the complication of keyless fusee winding." The subject is explored in more detail by Chamberlain in his book *It's about Time* in the chapter on "Development of the Motor Barrel". As he points out, American watchmakers used the going barrel from at least 1850 onwards but "The English makers continued the use of the fusee long after the French, Swiss and American makers had abandoned it". In fact it continued in England until a fairly abrupt change took place between 1880 and 1890. The transition is very clearly marked by the case dating of my nineteenth-century watches. It was a last-minute effort, reluctantly undertaken, to bring the English watch into line with foreign competition. It should be noted, however, that the prototype of the going barrel was being used in some Ormskirk verges about 1815 (see later, page 78).

Though the early examples of this phase, which extended from, say, 1880 to 1915, were key wound and key set, the centuries-old key was also on the point of demise. Though, of course, both examples of the fusee and the key continued to be made in lessening numbers into the twentieth century, keyless work was fairly abruptly adopted in this country in 1890. The changeover is again pinpointed by examples in my collection. At the same time side setting of the hands was adopted. At first this was simply a push-piece let into the shoulder of the case on either side of the stem. Later the push-piece was protected by solid faired-off shoulder olivettes. It is difficult to say whether a right or a left shoulder positioning gives the easiest setting, but in about 1900 sleeve hand setting ousted the side-set watch. The earliest going-barrel lever watch in my collection is a beautiful piece, a key wind watch by John Brownhill of 5 Prussia Street, Liverpool. It is well ahead of its time, being case dated 1872, whereas the next nearest date is 1889.

There is another feature in these movements to which little if any reference is made in the books—namely the dummy barrel. This is an empty replica of the going barrel, which occupies the space previously taken by the fusee. Tyler in his *Craft of the Clock Maker* notes the dummy barrel but probably is making a mistake in judging it to have no function other than to fill the space vacated by the fusee. While it is true that the dummy barrel is empty it should be noted that it meshes with the great wheel of the going barrel and in fact it transmits the power to the rest of the train as did the fusee. Were the dummy barrel absent winding would be clockwise. Not only would this be inconvenient but it would reverse the tradition of centuries. It looks as if the dummy barrel had a logical use after all and in some cases the height is cut down so that it really looks what it is in fact—a very thick wheel just as is found at the base of the fusee. In the majority of my key-wind going-barrel watches and movements the dummy barrel is present and winding is anti-clockwise. When the dummy is absent and the barrel geared direct to the trainwork winding may be either way. This, however, exposes the trainwork very directly to damage if the mainspring breaks when fully wound, hence the introduction of the patent safety pinion. It should be noted that both the verge and the fusee lever wind anti-clockwise when wound from the back of the movement. With keyless work it is essential that the winding button should not revolve as the mainspring unwinds; as other methods come into use and the dummy barrel disappears.

There are thirty examples of cased going-barrel English levers to be examined, together with eleven uncased movements (see illustrations Nos. 20–26). Owing to the rapid changes taking place during this period, there is a bewildering variety of design. This defies any simple classification and makes description very confusing, even when the chronographs are relegated to a separate section. The collector will find that there are still plenty of these pieces to be found in good condition and moderately priced. Though in many cases they do not appeal very much to me personally they should not be overlooked or rejected, for shortly they will be scarce. Their lack of appeal is simply that in attempts to make a cheap working-man's watch the grace of the mid-century fusee lever has been lost. We see heavily figured dials and clumsy cases. Perhaps the main dividing line is that of key-wind or keyless and on the whole the English makers still predominantly clung to the key-wind pattern. The exception to this is the use of the three-quarter plate movement which was usually linked with button wind and side set. These present usually between 1890 and 1915 and in my experience this is the pattern of the heavy gold case, commonly open faced, the stamp of the moneyed Edwardian gentleman who often bought such a piece from Benson of London. Only a few occurred in silver cases.

Among the more ordinary silver key-wind watches of this period dummy barrels were the rule rather than the exception. Two characteristic examples were almost a pair bought at the same time from the same shop and reputed to have been owned by two brothers (see illustration No. 23). They cost me £7 each and were hallmarked Birmingham 1897 and 1898, suggesting that they were a fully finished product of a Coventry factory and retailed by Russells of Liverpool. Certainly both dials were made by the same man and the movement numbers are close together. Both the cases were stamped T.R. (i.e., Thomas Russell) though it is doubtful whether the firm were ever casemakers. They may have been made by the nearby firm of Benson Bros. (B.B.) in Wood Street, Liverpool, which would make the Chester hallmark more likely. It is interesting that the hallmark on the stem is different from that on the watch case, suggesting they were made at that time by another firm and hallmarked separately. Both watches were in good condition though wear on the bow indicated a long usage. After overhaul there was good timekeeping and a healthy ringing tick.

The type of case used for these silver going-barrel levers was that known as the "double bottomed". The back opened by pressure on the push-piece on the stem disclosing a fixed dome pierced for winding and possibly also for hand setting. Usually, however, setting was still done by the square on the centre arbor. Almost invariably the back was decorated outside with the shield and garter motif. The bezel hinged at nine o'clock with the movement latch at six o'clock. The movement swung out from a top hinge and the standard dust cover was secured by the traditional semi-circular catch. On two of my covers there is an unusual circular catch the size of a silver threepenny piece, but this is very rarely seen. Locally these watches were usually engraved for Russells of Liverpool, but Graves of Sheffield was another large retailer. Judging from the hallmarks commonly seen, Coventry was largely outdistancing Prescot in these early days—to the ratio of Birmingham 15, London 9 and Chester only 4.

Russells of Liverpool is still trading, one of the very few firms to have survived from the heyday of the pocket watch era. There is a long and continuous record of the Russell family, starting when the son of Thomas Russell of Cumberland came to Lancaster to start his watchmaking apprenticeship in 1740. When his apprenticeship was finished he worked with Robert Gillow, supplying the movements for Gillow's long-case clocks. His son moved to Liverpool to manufacture Russell's Time-O-Day watches and in 1858 the firm was given the Royal Warrant by Queen Victoria. Thomas Russell, of the two watches mentioned above, built the main premises in Church Street but this was destroyed by bombing in 1940. At the present time the head of the firm is Mr. Tom Russell, the fifth generation, and he has been joined by the sixth generation in Mr. Barrie Russell. It must be very rare indeed to find commercial survival such as this through the many ups and downs that have plagued the watch trade. There are many examples of Russell's watches in the collection but none earlier than the 1890s.

This type of watch is still relatively easy to find but they are not very attractive to me though a group of twenty-five present for analysis. Owing to the mechanical changes in this period, description can be confusing. This was the Englishman's watch *par excellence*, solid and respectable, fighting the last hopeless battle against the foreign invasion. When in gold they have to be lodged in the bank because of their value. The retail price, for a good example, has now crept beyond the £200 mark and at this price there are naturally plenty for the collector to choose from. The gold cases clung to the side set rather than the sleeve even in the times when sleeves were common. The silver cases can also be massive, to the stage of being ugly, but there are many examples of the cheaper models. As might be anticipated, the three-quarter plate movements could reach a very high standard with fifteen jewels in the expensive watches. Looking at a group of movements which had survived after scrapping the gold cases, only one showed a clubfooted escape wheel. All the rest persisted with the English spur tooth and they were wound by individually made bevelled wheels. Keyless movements were usually pinned into the case and given an opening dome.

Those going-barrel levers which were still key wound could not, of course, accommodate the side setting mechanism for the hands. Of my twenty-five examples eight were key-wind, one as late as 1915. This type of watch was wound through the dome, the hands being set by the square on the centre arbor. The movements were hinged from the front to swing out and each had a close-fitting brass dust cover. Even when the change came to keyless work the winding arbor can often be on the back plate.

This last phase in English watchmaking is naturally a sad one. Dating the watches shows that starting about 1890 the trade was virtually dying by 1905 and dead by 1915. There was a growing demand for watches both here and abroad but the industry in this country was priced out of competition because it still used cottage industry methods in Lancashire and the small factory workshops in Coventry.

As far back as 1843 the British Watch Company was set up with John Barwise as chairman, the plan being to start a watch factory, the first in this country. However, the watchmaking trade successfully opposed, by Parliamentary action, its incorporation. This short-sighted action allowed the old methods to continue. What these methods were Dennison recorded from his own observations. He must have been describing those found at Prescot, where each of the many craftsmen concerned worked in his own home or small workshop; scattered over a wide area. Each passed the movement in its progressive growth from one place to the next with great inefficiency and waste of time. The most that could be attained was that the cheaper watches were processed in small batches. Eventually the basic movement emerged "in the grey", i.e., in unpolished brass. In Prescot this was a "rough" movement, in Continental terms the *ébauche*. This was then taken by coach to Liverpool to be finished (or more likely the tradesmen walked there). Though the results were very good the process was terribly labour-intensive and it is hinted that the tradesmen's drinking habits made them irregular. Probably the combination of poor wages and very exacting work fostered the drinking.

No unit was larger than a small workshop where the assembly of the *ébauche* took place. For centuries Prescot had functioned in this primitive way, supplying much of America's and most of England's needs in movements, material and tools. By about 1880, however, Prescot was beginning to decline, finding it difficult to understand how to adapt from the old ways. America was becoming self-sufficient and, perhaps more important, Coventry was organizing larger and more efficient workshops or even small factories. It was then that T. P. Hewitt (perhaps related to the Thomas Hewitt who was concerned with the abortive attempts to set up the British Watch Company) began his venture—the Lancashire Watch Company. Perhaps unfortunately, this was organized on the Waltham pattern. A large factory was built at Prescot and an attempt was made to carry out every step in manufacture under one roof. There were of course plenty of skilled tradesmen who had no alternative than to come into the factory.

The first watch was produced about 1893 and the factory finally failed in about 1910. It was a constant struggle to raise new capital, suggesting that the scheme had never been profitable. The main aim of the company—it passed under various titles—was the production (as can be seen in its catalogues) of the going-barrel English lever. Many were produced on the traditional lines in heavy gold and silver cases and as chronographs. But the great need was to succeed in selling cheaper watches for the working man and here the Prescot factory was beaten by the Waltham and Continental competition. The Lancashire Watch Company's John Bull watch at about five shillings neither carried the market nor produced enough profit. With the closure of the factory Prescot abdicated its long-held position. The one remaining watchmaker finally closed his shop in the 1960s. Some of his equipment and some relics of the factory are preserved in the Liverpool City Museum.

6

The Centre-seconds Chronograph

BEFORE discussing this type of watch we have to deal with matters of terminology. Strictly speaking a chronograph, as its name implies, is a watch or clock which traces a record on paper and produces a graph or at any rate writes. Such a movement was hardly, if ever, made so this is a misnomer to begin with. Nor is a chronograph a chronometer, a movement with a helical spring and a detent which was made in the middle of the nineteenth century for ordinary social use. They were fine watches but very costly to make, difficult to repair and were not self-starting. The result is that there are few to be found and I have never had the opportunity to afford one for my collection.

The Swiss today refer to their high-grade wrist watches as chronometers, but, of course, they cannot boast a real chronometer movement. Chronometer pocket watches, made from the middle of the eighteenth century to the early twentieth century were quite a different proposition. Centre seconds were used from quite early days though initially they were not common, just as the seconds dial and hand were not commonplace until the advent of the fusee lever. Though centre seconds hands (now called sweep seconds) had long been feasible they did not become popular as chronographs until the later years of the nineteenth century.

To sum up, the chronograph is a Victorian salesman's name for a centre seconds watch stop-work to give a rough estimate of elapsed time in seconds. When fitted with more elaborate stop-work it graduates to the level of an accurate stop-watch (see illustrations Nos. 29–36), and it must be admitted that, spanning as it does the phasing out of the key winding, it makes for some confusion in description.

The movements were always three-quarter plate, it is exceptional to find a half-plate. Until about 1890 the fusee was still used and the winding was by key. It is difficult on simple inspection to be certain of the fusee unless of course the movement is taken out of the case. It so happens that most of my silver-cased examples are key wound with a fusee movement. Those in gold cases and the uncased movements, which usually come from gold cases, have going barrels and keyless work. It looks as if the fashion started off at an everyday level and then graduated to an expensive fine-quality affair. The button wind had a solid stem-piece and usually worked by means of bevelled wheels. There was rarely sleeve hand-setting and the side hand-set was distinctive of the type.

The movement in the key-wind era did not swing out like the fusee levers though the hinge was often retained in the twelve o'clock position. The movement was pinned into the case by a peg at six o'clock. This meant that the dome, pierced for winding and hand-setting, was hinged as in the modern pocket watch. Taking the movement out is, therefore, not easy for the amateur.

The stop-work was always actuated by a flat sliding button on the body of the case at the two o'clock position. For stopping, a thin wire brake is pressed against the roller of the escapement. Though this is very simple it is hardly satisfactory. The button sticks down, and the sweep does not always restart, depending on the hope that there will be sufficient power left in the coiled hair-spring. The pocket chronograph has an 18,000 train and beats fifths of a second. The long sweep hand (which was always counterbalanced) reaches right to the edge of the dial, where the division is into 300 and numbered as such. On the better-class watches one pressure on the winding button brings the sweep to zero and the next starts it moving, while the third stops the hand—a much more positive method of timing. For stop-watch accuracy, i.e., true split-second work, a much more complicated mechanism, as described by Britten in *The Watch and Clockmakers Handbook* (1896), is needed.

The Swiss also made chronographs during this period, but my feeling is that they followed the English style rather than led the way. The examples that have come my way have not been of a very high standard.

These watches have always been a favourite of mine as examples of very high class workmanship and finish. I can draw upon twenty-eight examples and in addition the uncased movements are usually good, having come from heavy gold cases. On one occasion I was offered—at bullion value—a watch of this type in which the case weighed 7 ounces troy of 18ct. gold. Unfortunately I could not afford to buy it, for almost certainly it would have fallen victim to some vandal who would sell the case.

The cases were massive, size 20 or over and perhaps $2\frac{1}{2}$ inches in diameter. The frontispiece shows such a watch with traditional chain and medallion, being case-dated Birmingham 1888. In silver or gold the case weighed between 2 and 4 ounces—the weight sometimes to be found stamped on the case. Silver cases usually were given gold hinges. Heavier still were the hunters and demi-hunters. On the upper part of the dial usually appeared the legend "Centre Seconds

Chronograph" with the movement number. The retailer might write his name in the lower half but this was not usual as the watches were usually bought in fully made up by the Birmingham and Coventry makers whose name—Newsome, Drinkwater, Rotherham and Sons—was to be found under the dial. The Lancashire Watch Company also put out some good examples—the Alacrity movement for instance. The usual practice was for the retailer to have his name engraved on the top plate. Rolled gold cases were also popular and I have a very good example by Sewill of Liverpool, a firm who also handled and rated chronometers and are still in active business. Two Liverpool firms, Hargreaves and Kellie (neither extant), may possibly have been the actual makers of the watches engraved in their names. I have several very good examples of their work.

Chronographs were only fashionable over a very narrow period and few of mine fall outside the years 1880 to 1900. They epitomized the successful, if perhaps vulgar, ambition of the solid Victorian businessman. He might use a silver-cased version during the week and bring out the gold watch for Sunday wear.

One wonders what exactly the late Victorian gentlemen were aiming to time with their chronographs. There were no cars or aeroplanes, though no doubt speculators could time track and sports events fairly accurately. Doctors could use it to count the pulse impressively. Presumably its main use was to while away the time on a train journey and calculate what speed was being made between the distance posts. It was, however, the prestige watch to carry during those days, and carry would be the operative word! On weighing some of the silver chronographs, watch and movement could take the spring balance down to 7 or 8 ounces troy. The massive silver Albert could add another two or three ounces, so the wearer could be carrying half to three-quarters of a pound avoirdupois in his waistcoat pocket. However, if the owner was successful and well covered such an addition would hardly be noticed.

7

The English Fusee Lever

THE lever escapement was invented by Thomas Mudge in 1769. Perhaps the best account of its history is given by Clutton and Daniels in their standard text *Watches* (1965): "It is thus probably true to say that no more than two dozen English lever escapement watches survive from before 1800 . . . and after this no more was heard of the escapement in England for 15 years. When it was again taken up in England it was in Lancashire in quite cheap watches, and it did not fully regain its status as a high-grade escapement until 1850." Thus on the English scene the lever escapement was quite abruptly adopted after 1830 and the fusee went out of favour equally suddenly about 1880, production tapering off until 1900 when the going barrel had swept it away. As usual, the verges continued to be made alongside the levers much later into the twentieth century. Though Thomas Earnshaw, who died in 1829, was using lever escapement, the London trade took slowly to the innovation, and it is probably correct to say that it was not until the middle of the century that they were finally persuaded of its value. In the meantime it remains the escapement of choice for all pocket watches, the cylinder being Continental in its persistence and the chronometer watch escapement being very rarely seen. It still remains the mainstay of the Swiss wrist watch trade. In France, the development of the lever was under way before 1800.

It is remarkable that 1830 stands out in horological writing. Before this date there is extensive discussion of all the many attempts to find the ideal escapement. The lever attracts only passing attention and is never spotted as the eventual winner, while the verge soldiers on as the day-to-day watch. When in the early 1830s the lever emerged as the successor to the verge (a verdict since undisputed) it was really all over "bar the shouting". Strangely enough, however, there was no shouting, instead a very significant horological silence and very little has been written subsequently of the last hundred years of the pocket watch. Clutton and Daniels devote exactly one and a quarter pages to

"The Modern Watch, 1830 to 1960". Baillie ends his lists at 1825. In *Clocks and Watches, 1400 to 1900* (1967) Eric Bruton has one paragraph on "Late Watches". George Daniels in *English and American Watches* (1967) has a chapter on "The English Watch: Final Development and Decline". P. W. Cumhaill in *Investigating in Clocks and Watches* (1967) has a paragraph on "19th-century Watches". E. J. Tyler in *The Craft of the Clock Maker* (1973) has several pages of information on later watches. By far the majority of the space in *Antiquarian Horology* is devoted to the pre-1830 era. Only T. P. Camerer Cuss's *The Country Life Book of Watches* (1967), in the chapters on "The Lever Escapement" and "The Art and Mystery", gives us any useful account of nineteenth-century watches. Incidentally, the very complete glossary to this book is the most useful the beginner and the amateur can get hold of; unfortunately it is now probably out of print, but a new edition of de Carle's *Watch and Clock Encyclopedia* is available. It is unfortunate that there should be the lack of interest in watches that do not quite fall into the antique field, for it is here that today's collector will, in practice, largely be working.

When the lever took over from the verge it carried with it into the next sixty years the fusee and chain as motive power. As far as the fusee was concerned, this was in the verge a "plain fusee", i.e., there was no maintaining power. The "going fusee" was invented by John Harrison in 1750 and its use enabled the clock or watch to be wound without the danger of stopping or losing time during the winding process. It is not clear from Britten whether maintaining power was used in later verges—probably it was not. Certainly, however, it was used in the fusee lever, but again Britten is not clear whether this was so from the earliest days of these escapements. In regard to the chain there is a fascinating pamphlet by Allen White under the title of *The Chain Makers* (1967). The fusee itself was in the process of becoming much shallower to allow the case to be thinner and more elegant. The movements still swung out from a hinge above the dial but the brass dust cap now became universal. The bow lost its D form and became round, as in the very old watches. The movements remained full plate, and the balance remained outside the top plate. The ornate balance cock of the verge disappeared in favour of a straight plain cock on which was later mounted a plain index adjustment. The pair case was already beginning to give way to the single consular case and the hunting case was already established. Jewelling was found in all but the cheap movements. The balance wheel was taken over from the verge as a solid steel construction but it changed to brass and gold, eventually achieving timing studs though rarely the full divided bimetallic pattern.

By the 1850s the design was very much that of the modern watch (keyless work excepted) but later in the century there was a regression to the clumsy bulky watch. This period showed, therefore, quite important changes in the evolution of the modern pocket watch. It was also a time which saw the rise of the Coventry trade in the small factories scattered throughout the Midlands—though, in fact, my own collection does not reflect this in fusee levers. Coventry came well into the picture with the going barrel while Lancashire faded as if it could not bear "to see the back of the fusee watch". What is so remarkable in the history of the fusee lever is that the Prescot men, for reasons unknown to me, seem to have arrived at a simultaneous conclusion that the lever was the escapement of the future. They had little or no inspiration from Clerkenwell though this may have come from Continental sources after Waterloo. In taking this lead they ensured their livelihood for the next fifty years. Who the prime movers were we do not as yet know until the cryptic initials on the rough movements are personalised. Nor do we know to what extent those who finished and finally sold the detached levers (mainly in Liverpool) provided both the inspiration and the support.

For the purpose of study and illustration in this period there is a very good sample of over ninety complete watches and uncased movements (see illustrations Nos. 38–46). Largely these are drawn from the less expensive end of the range and are mostly in silver cases, and there is no evidence that any have been recased. The uncased movements have usually come (one assumes) from gold cases converted to bullion. The opportunity to recase such movements would largely not offer itself as at this period the cases were all hand made, with little standardization. It has been possible to restore all the complete watches to a reasonable standard of working order. This says a great deal for the original workmanship and it is still possible for the collector to find good specimens though the going price today (including V.A.T.) is about £30 for the silver watch. The best method for showing the popularity stakes for the making of these watches is to arrange by decades the case hallmarks, which have been stamped only in London, Chester and Birmingham. The following table shows the spread:

1834–1840	Six watches	—Chester 5, London 1, Birmingham 0
1841–1850	Three watches	—Chester 1, London 1, Birmingham 1
1851–1860	Three watches	—Chester 2, London 1, Birmingham 0
1861–1870	Eight watches	—Chester 4, London 3, Birmingham 1
1871–1880	Five watches	—Chester 2, London 2, Birmingham 1
1881–1890	Eight watches	—Chester 4, London 4, Birmingham 0
1891–1900	Six watches	—Chester 5, London 0, Birmingham 1
1912	One watch	—Chester 1.

So we see Lancashire making the major contribution, having the cases assayed at nearby Chester, and contributing 25 examples. London with 12 hallmarks comes in mainly between 1860 and 1890 and after that dropping the fusee. Birmingham, with only 4 attributions, hardly enters the field. As far as uncased movements are concerned, scrutiny of these for dating is quite unhelpful for they fall into the post-1825 silence. We are also now in the faceless country of the nineteenth century when the name written on the dial or engraved on the top plate is usually that of a retailer and there is little or no indication of the real maker. Quite a few were sold by large houses in Manchester such as Samuel (reputed to be a lady), Meyer, Wise, Rosenberg and Pomfret. In Liverpool there were Russells, Butterfield, Howard and Phillips. London supplies good examples by Savoury, Forrest and Benson.

The more reputable Liverpool makers, i.e., those who had a considerable hand in the rebuilding and finishing of the movement, flourished in the 1830s and 1840s. Some of these appear in Baillie, usually because they were in business before as well as after 1825. Perhaps the leading light is Robert Roskell the younger—1830 onwards—who contributes a perfect gold-cased catch, case-dated ? 1850, and having a classical gold face and raised gold numerals. Another watch by the same firm is in silver with a plain face (1875)—there is also an uncased movement. A similar watch with a gold decorated dial is by Hester Mason of Liverpool. Silver decorated dials with raised gold numerals in silver cases are to be found in this period. These dials are very difficult to restore and clean because of accumulation of dirt in the engraving. Richard Hornby is the maker of my earliest fusee lever (case-dated 1834). Baillie dates him as 1810 to 1829 but, as we shall see later, this does not mean that he died or went out of business in 1829—more probably he ceased to remain a member of the Clockmakers Company. Britten records that he lived in Pool Lane, Liverpool, from 1810 to 1830. A James Hornby of Liverpool (1803 to 1829) is represented by two uncased movements. A William Bellion produced a watch case-dated 1867 and a similar uncased movement. Several movements were finished in Preston and quite uniquely in my collection there is a movement from Dublin signed by John Donegan.

In some of these watches there was no jewelling apart, of course, from the balance staff. However, with so many Liverpool examples in the collection there are several which show typical Liverpool jewelling or, more coarsely, Liverpool windows. Usually these jewels are of quartz but sometimes the customer would specify natural rubies. One such is a well-finished movement by James Hornby which is still running sweetly under my eye without any overhauling, though it is lacking a dial. Examples of this form of jewelling are shown in illustrations 108–110. One or, more frequently, three of the top plate holes (and occasionally the fusee arbor) are given massive jewels. In the James Hornby example these are mounted in brass caps with small retaining screws. Though these "windows" are rather hidden under the rim of the balance wheel they do give the movement a striking and expensive look. Any idea that they have a longer life or add efficiency is, of course, erroneous. Usually, if one inspects the bottom plate, the jewels are much smaller, even of normal size. This local idiosyncrasy was probably simply a sales gimmick, a hallmark, as it were, of the Liverpool gentleman. Presumably the large jewels were inserted by the Prescot jeweller or this could have been done by the Liverpool maker when he finished the movement. In view of the trade out of the port of Liverpool many such movements, enhanced or plain, must have found their way to America. Indeed, up to the rise of the Coventry trade, Prescot supplied most of this country with rough movements. Many would have been exported as such, possibly even to the Continent since tradition suggests that there was quite a brisk trade from and to Prescot across the Channel.

Among other points to be noted in the fusee lever, the elegance and slimness of the case (again a Continental trend) has already been noted. It is difficult to imagine a fusee lever in a pair case and I have no example of one in the collection The gold watches with decorated dials are particularly elegant (see illustration No. 45); they are on the whole small enough to be used as a dress watch or even a lady's watch. Since the hands usually found are black or blued, they are not easy to read. Such watches are still available to the collector though naturally costly. One could speculate, however, that the price in pounds today would not be so very different from the original cost in the pounds of over a century ago. The traditional design of the hands of the fusee lever was that of the fleur-de-lys on both minute and hour hand (see illustrations). Later perhaps the hour hand was likely to be plain. Unfortunately, when the hands had to be replaced, spades might well be used and they might not always be a match. It is difficult, unless one has long experience, to be sure whether the hands on watches as old as this are original and of the contemporary fashion. In true conservatism the hands on two watches, dated 1897 and 1912, are still classic fleur-de-lys. In earlier watches of this period gold hands were common but as the century progressed they began to be replaced by blued steel to make reading easier. As illustrations show, the classic dial was attractively written with slim and tall numerals. The seconds dial, though not unknown in verges, became increasingly common with the lever watch. At first it was rather larger than we are accustomed to find on the modern watch dial, but this gave the makers an opportunity to design it tastefully.

As has been noted the balance cock from the beginning of this period departed from the verge tradition of being ornate and pierced and covering the whole balance wheel. The shape was now plain and finger-shaped, showing most of the balance though varying degrees of decorative engraving was still used. The index in the early days might still continue the verge fashion and be under the balance wheel and moving along an engraved quadrant on the top plate. It seemed to be a Liverpool tradition to engrave the town name in Gothic characters surrounded by scrolls. Perhaps this was all done by one firm of plate engravers—the maker's name was commonly in flowing script. What puzzles me in these early Liverpool watches is the frequent engraving of the word PATENT across the foot of the cock. The earliest watch, by Will. Rowley of Liverpool (not in Baillie) is hallmarked Chester 1834. The cock shows the words PATENT DETACHED. The use of the word "patent" appears similarly on Litherland's rack levers. This was justified, since Peter Litherland did in fact patent his escapement in 1791. To use the words DETACHED PATENT would be very correct but the word PATENT is probably not to be taken in its legal sense but is used for sales promotion.

Chamberlain in *It's About Time*, a record of much research, remains unclear on this point also. Initially he says: "I am unable to learn what the impetus was which in the middle of the nineteenth-century turned the whole watchmaking world toward the detached lever." After noting the popularity of the duplex and chronometer in London, the cylinder (among others) in France and Switzerland, and the rack lever in Liverpool, he goes on as follows: "I judge that in Liverpool the term lever escapement was applied to the rack lever, for on many of the early *free* lever escapements are the following words, 'detached lever escapement'. Within my memory I have heard old watchmakers speak of it as the patent lever. There was of course, *no patent on the escapement as a whole*, but several on special features of the fork action. A tradition has grown up, quite ingenious but entirely at variance with fact, that the free lever was the outgrowth of the rack lever and all but one of the leaves of the pinion. The rack lever, however, so popular in the Liverpool market did perform the valuable service of making a vast number of people familiar with many of the features contained in the lever escapement."

There were, of course, several, if not many, other inventors who took out patents for their escapements. Was there, however, any specific person who invented and patented the detached lever escapement by the Lancashire makers the idea may have been imported *in toto* from the Continent; or the adoption may have been by concensus among the various movement builders in the town. have been by concensus among the various movement builders in the town. The literature available to me does not clear this point. What we do know by hearsay from the later generations of Prescot men is that, not unnaturally, since it was a small place, there was a good deal of professional jealousy.

Moreover, each individual craftsman stuck rigidly to his small specialty and was very loath to part with the secrets and techniques of his trade—hence the reluctance to abandon the fusee in the 1880s in favour of the going barrel. The fusee makers would have lost their livelihood and be reluctant to learn the new technique. The Prescot men, being a very clannish lot rightly considered themselves the elite. Strangers were given a very cold shoulder and this was still the case when in the ruin of the local trade they had to move to Liverpool and Manchester and become repairers.

The fusee lever period in English watchmaking would seem then to be quite significant though largely ignored by most horological writers. It was introduced at a crucial time for the English trade. Throughout the eighteenth century English verges had held their own both at home and abroad and their reputation was high despite the strong French competition. However, in spite of much inventiveness no successor to the verge was in sight at the beginning of the nineteenth century. The French, and later the Swiss, thought that the future lay with the cylinder escapement and probably did not give their own work on the lever enough consideration. The cylinder did not stay the course either in the cheap version or the more expensive. The English makers also thought highly of the cylinder, the duplex was a simple and reliable construction, the rack lever was acceptable but provincial, while the Ormskirk verge was truly rural. None of these, nor the even more complicated escapements was the long-term answer since they all offered greater or lesser degrees of frictional rest. To quote Chamberlain (who was an engineer), "... the most ideal conditions for a balance or pendulum should embrace freedom to swing without external interference, or as little as possible". This, of course, was the underlying ideal towards which all watchmakers were striving. With the detached lever (and its subsequent improvement of "draw") the goal had been reached, a fact that history has completely confirmed. It was upon the basis of the "English lever" (either fusee or going barrel) and its accepted worldwide reputation that our watch trade survived and prospered for the next seventy or eighty years until killed by the machine-made watch.

8
The Verge

IN comparison with the space devoted in the horological literature to unusual experimental escapements relatively little is said about the verge itself and much of the attention is focused on its decorative side. This is an injustice, for the verge escapement had been the workhorse of the watch from its earliest beginnings in the sixteenth century and it continued to be made even after 1850. It had a run, therefore, of over three hundred years and continued serenely through the challenge of many innovations. Its continued popularity must have been based on a solid reputation of longevity, reliability, repairability and adequate timekeeping. Obviously in the early phase it was very crude, hardly better than a pocket sundial, but of course it was a man's first attempt to provide portable time.

Improvement depended on several important steps. The provision of a watch glass at an early stage. The introduction of the fusee about 1525—the inventor of which is unknown. Subsequently the fusee chain replaced catgut lines. Then, about the middle of the seventeenth century, the balance spring initiated by Hook and applied by Tompion, was generally adopted and the "sprung" verge had a chance of reasonable accuracy. A little later jewelling became available thus lengthening the life of the pivot holes. It was on the basis of these four main steps forward that the verge reached a useful time keeping standard. It was simple to repair and lasted for generations. Significantly, all but a very few of my verges have been restored to working order after a long working life which started centuries ago. The mechanism of the verge is so simple that little attention is given to it in the horological texts in comparison with that spent on the rare and the exotic variations.

The best account of the verge escapement and its modifications is given by Chamberlain in his *It's About Time*. As far as the collector is concerned it is at the present day not easy to enter the verge field purely because of the high prices of the ordinary pieces. There are, however, still many verge watches available, the common or garden silver nineteenth-century watch being priced at between fifty and sixty pounds today. Older and choicer pieces are considerably dearer, of course, but they are still easily found. Study of the auction price lists suggests, however, that verges by good makers remain reasonably steady and have not escalated in anything like the same fashion as have clocks by the same makers. For the investor, as opposed to the collector, the good verge is still a sound buy and looks as if it will always hold its price and rise with inflation.

For my part, it has been possible to build up a reasonably representative body of verges on the dual basis of having bought them when they were cheaper and not venturing far above the commonplace everyday level. Only one is in fact cased in gold. Nevertheless the range is large enough in numbers and wide enough in dating to show all the salient points. Extreme antiquity, leading names among makers, artistic and colourful decoration are not represented on the grounds of cost. All these points are well covered in several standard texts. The youngest piece is case-dated 1875 and the oldest is about 1720. Between these dates the ground is evenly covered. It would have been pleasant to have gone back to the days beyond 1720 but, as one would expect, survivors from those times are relatively rare and remain museum specimens. For my part, it took a long time before it was possible to advance my collecting beyond 1800, though eventually these began to come my way. The scope and quality of my antique watches are, of course, very modest when compared with that of experts who started earlier and worked more assiduously. Looked at, however, from the opposite point of view, that of the man who is collecting under present-day conditions, it still seems remarkable that one was able to get so far. It enables me to speak of about a hundred cased and uncased movements of this type without counting the rarer escapements which are the subject of another chapter. For the sake of clarity and to avoid repetition, where possible the material has been considered in three groups—the nineteenth-century verge, the characteristic late eighteenth-century verge, and the early eighteenth-century verge. The basis for what may be thought of as quite arbitrary divisions is that some quite striking modifications of the form of the verge took place round 1800; while at the other end of the century the verge in 1700 was a rather crude affair awaiting the civilization and precision which overtook it between 1725 and 1750.

9

The Nineteenth-century Verge

It is perhaps heartening to find that among the fifty or so watches and movements subsequent to 1800 (see illustrations Nos. 47–58) there are twenty-seven which warrant recognition by Baillie. Twenty, however, do not merit a mention, some of which will, of course, have been made subsequent to 1825. Another twelve are unnamed. The general trend in the group is as one could expect—even after Britten's list for the London makers (up to 1895) had been consulted. The unidentified and the anonymous makers clustered at the more modern end of the spectrum and the accredited makers were nearer to the eighteenth century. The hallmarking of these silver case watches is probably pretty reliable. They are unlikely to be recased since there is nothing unusual or outstanding in the movements. Analysis of case dates was therefore able to give a reasonably accurate endpoint in the decline of the verge, as the following table shows:

Hallmark	No. of watches	Hallmark	No. of watches
1800–1805	Six	1836–1840	Four
1806–1810	Six	1841–1845	Two
1811–1815	Five	1846–1850	None
1816–1820	Four	1851–1855	None
1821–1825	Four	1856–1860	Two
1826–1830	Five	1861–1875	Two
1831–1835	Three		

It can be seen that after 1840 the output of verges drastically declined, and here again we see on the opposite side of the coin the effect of the introduction of the detached lever after 1830. This is an unusually swift change for horological fashion. Usually there is a long overlap compounded both of customer loyalty and trade inertia. This sudden downfall of an escapement that had held its own despite criticism for over three hundred years speaks not only for the sterling service given by the verge but also for overt superiority of its successor. It was as if the verge had ploughed steadily on through the last hundred years of its life resisting the challenge of many would-be supplanters until the real heir appeared.

The verge entered the nineteenth century in what seems to me to have been the form of a civilized watch. It was small, neat, accurate enough, and in good taste. However, only the comparatively rich could afford it and they influenced the design. Competition from France had been stifled by the Napoleonic wars. During the short intervals of peace visitors to France could buy the Continental watches, but again these were strictly for the carriage trade. Industrialization and the wartime prosperity created another market, of a lower taste, which demanded substantial pieces, so the more numerous commonplace watch grew larger and heavier. The pendant, for example, became wide and flattened and very solid. The bow was deeper and heavier. The pair cases were clumsy but continued to be used to the end of the verge era. However, in the early 1800s the single consular case, named for Napoleon by French watchmakers, found its way over from the Continent. A characteristic example was made by Matt Hick of York, hallmarked London 1823 (Baillie's dates 1812 to 1834). It is single-cased with a solid round bow, the case being plain undecorated silver. Large and heavy, it is of admirable workmanship and timekeeping—just the thing for a plain-speaking Yorkshireman to wear but quite devoid of any pretence of artistic taste. As illustration No. 54 shows, Matt Hick was conservative in the movement, continuing the decorated round cock though he had abandoned Tompion's rosette regulation. While there was considerable room for variation in design and actual size in the nineteenth-century verge, the workaday pattern such as is most likely to be found is instantly recognized as the clumsy pair case in silver.

The development of the single case allowed the casemakers to make a full hunting case or a half-hunter. The main technical problem here was devising a low-profile glass or crystal that would fit under the front metal flap (in contrast to the thick high dome glass used previously). Without a glass dust would be a great problem. It looks as if the hunter crystal was not available until later in the century. The full hunter opened on to the dial direct. A better alternative was the half-hunter with a sight glass which magnified a small central numeral chapter as in illustration No. 52. There is a romantic story that Napoleon made the first demi-hunter case by imperiously cutting out the centre of a full hunter cover with his penknife.

Another advance by the casemakers, dating again from about 1800, was the ability to bring the hinge of the outer pair case into the general outline. The casemakers seemed to have discarded the proud hinge so characteristic of the eighteenth-century case quite quickly. They were able to move smoothly to that most complicated case, the fusee lever hunter. Here they had to accommodate three hinges—those of the frontal flap, the crystal glass and the movement hinge.

Another advance was a change of the regulator style. In the eighteenth-century verges this was universally the Tompion rosette. Now it became usual to place an index arm acting on the balance spring underneath the balance wheel. The end of the longer arm of the index moved along or across an arc engraved on the top plate. For the first time one end of the arc was marked Fast and the other Slow in a simple fashion. Another feature that disappeared after 1800 was the worm screw (tangent screw) used for setting up the mainspring. Maintaining power was, I think, neither used nor needed in a verge. In the transition phase of this change the place previously occupied by Tompion's rosette was filled by a domed and usually blued blank, as is shown in illustration No. 55.

Another significant change was the introduction of the unsigned movement. All my eighteenth-century watches and movements were meticulously signed. The tradition was that the fullness of the attribution was governed by the quality of the watch. If the maker was proud of it he had it written in full—Edward Jones, No. 12 The Strand, London. If not so pleased the label would be Edw. Jones, Strand, London. Lower down the scale it would be Jones, Strand, London; while the cheapest, but still signed watch, would be simply (and unidentifiably) Jones, London. Rather than leave the watch unsigned at all the very basic watches might carry a pseudonym. However, among my forty-three cased nineteenth-century verges there are ten unsigned watches, the earliest appearing in 1801. Mostly they appear between 1825 and 1845, and contrary to what might be expected there are eight London hallmarks (against one from Chester and one from Birmingham), so presumably these movements came mainly from Clerkenwell. They are plain everyday serviceable watches for people who did not want to pay extra to have a watch by a named maker. It should perhaps be mentioned that the practice of writing the maker's or the retailer's name on the dial was not common usage either in the eighteenth or early nineteenth centuries though it was universal or at least usual in clock dials. In the early eighteenth century the maker's name was commonly engraved on the metal dial, as the metal offered a good opportunity for this. My leverized watch by Thos. Earnshaw had his name on the dial, but this was outstandingly rare practice until it became universal in the later decades of the last century. The painted dial often survives from about 1850. Illustration No. 49 shows the characteristic Farmer's Watch. This was sold by Wm. Tanner of Lewes and is case-dated London 1859. Dutch scenes, maritime pictures and other aspects of country life are also to be found.

The type of verge the collector is most likely to acquire in this nineteenth-century period is the ungainly silver pair case. This is sometimes thought of as the countryman's verge since he was more likely to be conservative and reject the new-fangled levers and single cases. Recently a very good example came my way (illustrations Nos. 47 and 48). It is in silver, pair cased, with an over-all outside diameter of 2¼ inches. The case is stamped as containing a weight of 3 ounces. Though there is a fair amount of wear on the bow pin the whole piece is in excellent condition. The bull's-eye glass is only moderately scratched, the hands are gold and original and the dial unmarked. The numerals are large, deep and forthright. Unusually, for this date, the hinge is old-fashionedly still outstanding. The case-dating is Birmingham 1847. There is a dust cover. The movement is signed J. Jarvis, Whitchurch (Baillie—early nineteenth century). There are six watch papers, all of John Jarvis, Watchmaker, Whitchurch. On the back of the papers in copperplate writing is the owner's name—Mr. Davies, Park Farm, Cholmondly (variously spelt), a village near Whitchurch. The dates are between 1874 and 1885. In writing the dates the year is sometimes put first, e.g., 76,11,7. The movement is a traditional verge retaining the round decorated cock, a plain top plate, and using Bosley's regulator.

This then is certainly a countryman's or farmer's watch and one can understand why painted dials were used to encourage sales. The Birmingham hallmark has an immediate significance. Whitchurch is within twenty miles of Chester but the watch was not submitted to assay there, the presumption being that the movement was not made in Lancashire. The likelihood is that watch and case were made in one of the small Coventry factories and merely retailed by the Whitchurch watchmaker. The rise of the Coventry trade in the later part of the nineteenth century was based on a much better developed factory system than the cottage industry methods of Prescot. It seems likely to me that the downfall of Prescot was as much due to its inability to cope with Coventry as to the later influx of American and Swiss machine-made watches.

It is never of much help to the collector to read about the unique, for the obvious reason that he will never personally meet it, but it is impossible to resist the temptation to describe the verge to end all verges. It was purely by chance that on my way out of an antique shop this goliath caught my eye as it hung among the pieces of plate. In diameter it was at least 3 inches and the case contained 7½ ounces of silver. The attribution is complicated. It was signed Morris Tobias of London and Liverpool, to whom Baillie gives dates of 1794 to 1812; he was a prestige maker of chronometers. The firm, in Wapping and the Minories, passed through several designations. Britten has a note of T. Morris of 68 Bell Dock, Wapping, 1794. What then are we to make of the Chester hallmark of 1868? There is also another name on the movement—that of Wm.

Taylor. At least three men of this name are noted by Baillie as being in Liverpool and each is given the same date of 1825.

The heavy case is single and the round heavy bow shows no marks of chain wear. Indeed it is hard to see how anyone would gladly carry such a heavy watch round in his waistcoat pocket. Similarly the movement is in pristine condition with no signs of wear, though a new spring had to be provided on routine overhaul. The movement is of very high standard and fully jewelled. Its period is entirely that of the last verges corresponding to the case-date of 1868. It may have been an apprentice piece, yet the finish suggests it was one of a "regular line" of retail supply. Morris Tobias is noted by Baillie as having patented a "sea clock". Certainly the size and weight of this piece is in keeping with a deck watch, i.e., the watch used to convey the ship's chronometer time to the deck when sextant observations were being taken. Subsequent reference to Charles Aked's *A Complete list of English Horological Patents up to 1853* (1975) confirms this. Patent No. 3584 of 16 July, 1812 shows "Tobias Morris—Binnacle timepiece or timekeeper". It therefore looks as if the firm of Morris Tobias continued to supply the movements until at least 1868 and that it was cased in Liverpool, with which town the firm and its ramifications were known to have connections. It seems unlikely that such a watch would be kept on deck by or in the binnacle housing as there would be little shelter for it. It would be kept securely in the Captain's cabin or charthouse and be carried on deck when needed for sextant work.

In all these notes as to the changes made in verges during the nineteenth century it will not have escaped notice that little has been said about the verge escapement and movement itself. This is because the fundamentals and movement design changed so little over 300 years that it was, and is, assumed that everybody fully understands the verge. Diagrams and brief explanations are to be found in all the standard texts on this basis and it would be a waste of time to repeat them here. Clutton and Daniels (*Watches*) give an illustration of the usual arrangement of the escapement between the plates. They say: "With pallets finally set at 100 degrees to 105 degrees the escapement continued in use for a further 200 years and resisted all efforts at refinement. If jewelled and very carefully made it would, for a few months, show a fairly consistent rate; but with the thickening of the oil the rate deteriorated so that it was inferior to that of a plain unjewelled escapement which would, by virtue of its many compensating inefficiencies, keep an indifferently close rate for many years without any attention." It would seem that the authors have here put their fingers on a very important point in the popularity of the verge, i.e., that the plain verge needed very little expert attention, and moreover the performance was adequate for that day and age.

It might be noted here that Greenwich Mean Time only became legal and official in this country in the year 1880. But even after that, until 1916, the time standard used by the whole of Ireland was that of local time at Dublin. Before 1880 each place used a time standard based on solar time, i.e., sundial time on a sundial set to the local longitude. There was no attempt at time zoning and a table of the differences between the principal places in this country and throughout the world is carried by Britten in his *Former Clock and Watch Makers* in the original edition of 1894. As explained by Eric Bruton (in *Clocks and Watches, 1400 to 1900*) this was inconvenient to coach travellers so that coaches worked to their own time tables. With the coming of more rapid travel by rail, about 1830, individual companies likewise set up their own railway time and eventually agreed on standardized railway time based on the G.W.R. at Swindon. The railways agreed to accept G.M.T. when it was introduced in 1880 and in 1884 the rest of the world (with the exception of Ireland and France) followed suit. Clearly, whatever the failings of the individual verge might be during the whole of the period that it was in production, the owner had to contend with the vagaries of local time, coach time and railway time. This must have involved everybody, whether they travelled or not, in some very complicated mental arithmetic—a process much more liable to gross error than the gaining or losing error of the verge itself.

In the early days of the verge, when reliable public clocks were rare, watches would be rated by the fixed sundial (if one was available) and set for local time. Britten (in the sixth edition, 1932) has a note on portable or pocket sundials in general use in the sixteenth and seventeenth centuries for this purpose. The commonest was a simple ring that could be carried in the pocket, but the more reliable carried a small compass for alignment of the magnetic North. The underlying interest of such instruments is that they transferred solar time to the watch in a way that was available in the pocket day or night. By the eighteenth century the verge had become reliable enough to stand on its own feet.

It might be helpful to collectors, however banal this may seem to the horologist proper, to make a list of the named watches and movements in my collection of nineteenth-century verges.

Name	Address	Hallmark	Baillie/Britten
		Cased Watches	
Ant. Shepperly	Nottingham	London 1820	1814–1818
T. Strong	London	London 1803	c.1800–1829
Underhill	Newport	Birmingham 1813	Late 18th C.
Peter Grayhurst	London	London 1802	1802–1830

Name	Address	Hallmark	Baillie/Britten
H. Wilson	London	London 1846	Early 19th C.
Wm. Tanner	Lewes	London 1859	——
Jno. Manders	Hitchin	Birmingham 1847	——
Wm. Terry	Richmond, Yorks	London 1801	b. 1774, d. 1848
Rob. Bowman	London	London 1826	——
Matt. Hick	York	London 1823	1812–1834
M. Tyson	Gosforth	Birmingham 1839	——
H. Nelson	London	London 1810	——
Thos. Mawkes	Derby	Birmingham 1814	——
Sam. Underhill	Wolverhampton	Birmingham 1829	——
Robt. Bowman	London	London 1837	——
Wm. Upjohn	London	London 1811	c.1800
Walley & Jones	Liverpool	Chester 1830	1785 onwards
Wm. Chamberlain	——	Birmingham 1835	——
Thos. Edwards	Corwen	London 1822	? Early 19th C.
J. Newton	London	London 1824	1815–1824
T. W. Field	Aylesbury	London	c.1800
Kirkwood	London	London 1807	——
N. Preston	London	London 1807	*ante* 1808
Thos. Startedoe	Cowes	London 1813	——
Hendrick	Droitwich	Birmingham 1835	——
Lewis	Bilston	Birmingham 1846	——
John Richardson	London	London 1803	London 1798
Norton	London	?Birmingham 1836	——
G. Gregson	London	London 1818	——
P. Richards	Liverpool	London 1829	——
Snow	Otley	London 1809	1780–1822
Fairclough	Liverpool	Chester 1816	1774–1803
Morris Tobias	London & Liverpool	Chester 1868	1794–1840
J. Jarvis	Whitchurch	Birmingham 1847	Early 18th C.
Richard Ward	London	London 1817	1835–1842

Uncased Movements

Name	Address	Hallmark	Baillie/Britten
Robt. Jones	Ruthin	——	c.1800
Robt. Hall	Oswestry	——	——
Johnson	Liverpool	——	? 1800–1809
H. Jackson	Newcastle	——	——
Cameron	Liverpool	——	c.1800

Name	Address	Hallmark	Baillie/Britten
Robt. Bowman	London	——	*c.*1830
John Edwards	London	——	1820–1830
Thos. Stanton	Oswestry	——	——
Moor & Sons	Hastings	——	——
Rich. Butt	Plymouth	——	——
Geo. Jeffreys	London	——	End 18th C.
Payne	London	——	——
J. Wright	London	——	1820–1830
Hayden	London	——	——
N. Preston	London	——	*ante* 1808

10

The Later Eighteenth-century Verge

BETWEEN the years 1740 and 1800 the design and fashion of the verge settled down to a constant and unvaried pattern that to me is the epitome of the verge style. In the early part of the period the outline was still large and globular, while after 1800 the shape was rather that of the mince pie or Eccles cake. In the period under discussion, however, the watch had become the smallest in diameter of all verge styles. Though this reduced the depth in proportion it still remained rather globular. It is not easy to convey the roundness in close-up photography but the illustrations do show the deepish bowl of the inner case as well as the wide spacing between the plates (see illustrations Nos. 59–77). This was largely due to retention of the tall form of the fusee and added to by the high cambered glass. They are, however, well-proportioned good-looking pieces and, as has been suggested previously, their good taste reflected that of the owners who would have been people of "quality". The workmanship of the movements was equally high-class and it is interesting to note that Clutton and Daniels regard 1850 as the birth year of the precision watch. The bulk of my forty cased watches and movements are *post*-1850, though some of the undated movements could be of earlier date. It has been possible to bring all the cased watches into working order and many of the movements ripped from gold cases are working spontaneously. It might be stressed again that cased or uncased they are all of one pattern, so that the watches of this period are instantly recognizable. This determined conservation of fashion is rather unusual at any period; usually there was somebody prepared to step out of the accepted line. The period was in fact one of great horological experimentation, but if we are to accept the evidence of the frequency of survival from those days, what people were actually buying was the sedate verge. Despite the heated arguments about the more expensive cylinder and the less expensive duplex (not to mention the *post*-1800 escapements) the verge remained the popular reliable watch. Nevertheless as far as today's collector is concerned he is beset both by cost and scarcity.

None of my cased watches reached the dignity of a gold case and most are in plain silver. Several are in pinchbeck or gilt, often worn, and lacking a hallmark. One has an outer case of tortoiseshell which has stood up to the years well. This was quite a usual finish to the high grade watch. Another common finish was that of shagreen, which in its true and natural state is the skin of the shark dyed green. Both tortoiseshell and shagreen had to be pinned or wired to the outer case by a pattern of silver or copper staples. Occasionally a third case is found outside.

The most outstanding feature of the outer case is the hinge which stands proud of the watch circumference. It is true that the upper and lower corners are chamfered (at an earlier date they were square), but it was not until 1800 that the casemakers managed to smooth the hinge away altogether. The bow is universally of a shallow D-shape pinned to the thin rounded pendant which generally turns. The small watch glasses with a bull's-eye flat are very hard to find now and I am personally reluctant to buy when this is missing, cracked or much scratched with wear. Metal dials had now been replaced with the white dial. These are necessarily small and difficult to read. In the course of time many of them are apt to show chips and cracks. The chips can be improved by filling in and the cracks made less obvious by careful soaking in detergent which washes out the dirt. The main numeral chapter is always in short Roman figures. Commonly, however, there is outside this another ring in which the minutes, at five-minute intervals, are lettered in Arabic numerals. This outer chapter began to disappear towards the end of the century. It is shown in several of the illustrations. A variant, possibly a phase in the transition, was that the Arabic numerals were only placed at the quarter-hours.

When we come to consider the types of hands used in the watches of this period we find that considerably less attention has been given to them than has been focused upon clock hands and long-case clock hands in particular. In de Carle's *Watch and Clock Encyclopedia* there is a very considerable list of hand styles, though biased towards the more modern end of the spectrum. There is, however, in the addendum, a shorter list of antique watch hands, from 1675 to 1885. Most of the hands found in my eighteenth-century watches and movements are illustrated in this second list. By far the most common through the whole period, and probably in the previous century, was some variant of the traditional "beetle and poker" design. These can be seen in illustrations to confer upon the dial a great sense of antiquity but one is surprised that eighteenth-century good taste tolerated them for so long. The dial is in any case small and rather cluttered, and the matt black over-elaborate hands do not make for easy reading. In other words, the beetle-and-poker hardly suited the elegance of the rest of the watch. Towards the end of the eighteenth century they began to be replaced by more pleasing patterns in gold as shown in de Carle's antique list. A not uncommon one was that of the double arrow, while occasionally rather fussy pierced hands are found. In my only French verge the hands are large and of intricate pattern embellished with diamanté. At the other end of the scale, however, some of the French designs were simple and in very good taste, e.g., those favoured by Breguet. The English designs were invariably restrained and were moving towards the spade which in the next century became almost universal. At first the spade was restricted to the hour hand with the minute hand discreetly swelled or possibly carrying a very small spade tip. However, as has been mentioned elsewhere, watch hands are fragile and have often been replaced at a later date by a style out of keeping with that of the dial. In most of my restored pieces, however, the original hands survived, in contrast to the uncased movements where the hands have often disappeared as a result of cannibalization.

Looking at the movements one is immediately struck by their relative depth in comparison with the breadth. In the earlier examples this is even more striking, as if there was a sudden over-violent swing from the large globular watch to the small round shape. One or two have well-designed dust covers (see illustration No. 97). The cover catch is the same as used in the next century with a raised piece for the balance cock. There is access to the winding arbor and the regulating rosette without the need to remove the dust cover. What all the movements show is a very high standard of workmanship, finish, gilding and decoration, and they fit very neatly into the small cases. They are very fully engraved, usually in flowing script, with the maker's name and address, in accordance with the Act of 1777. The balance cocks are triumphs of design, many of them fully pierced even to the foot of the cock.

Perhaps a more detailed description of a typical example would be allowable. The maker is Rt. Green of Liverpool who seems to have been quite prolific and for whom Baillie gives the single date of 1767. Britten notes several other Robert Greens of about the same period but not of Liverpool. The shape of the watch is that of the usual small flattened tangerine, and the hinge is external. The outer case is unusually copper gilt much worn in the exposed places. It is covered with natural shagreen stitched in place with two rows of copper wire. The plain inner case is in silver and pierced for winding, with a hallmark of London 1739. The hands are modern and incongruous—hence no photograph. The cock is pierced and engraved to the foot, showing a bird which might by a stretch of the imagination be the liver bird. The pillars are plain baluster as was common through the century. Regulation is by steel rosette numbered up to six. Like most eighteenth-century movements, the mainspring is set up by a worm screw device (tangent screw) on the pillar plate near the hinge. Despite the amount of wear shown by the shagreen cover, after overhaul the movement runs steadily with a reasonable rating on the bench. It might well have had a hundred years of working life or even longer. Adjustment of the setting-up was often so necessary that the makers provided a squared head so that the owner himself could use his own key for this purpose.

The makers of the forty watches and movements (all were signed) shows a significant geographical distribution. Rather over half (twenty-one) were from London makers. Liverpool makers numbered eight, while other Lancashire towns produced four. Birmingham, Aber, Odiham, Woodbridge, etc., had only one each.

Name	Address	Hallmark	Baillie/Britten
Cased Watches			
Hen. Aspinal	Liverpool	Chester 1787	1790–96
Wm. Jones	Aber	Birmingham 1797	——
Richard Gibb	London	London ——	1745
Thos. Dale	London	London 1745	c.1700
Rob. Innes	London	London 1750	*ante* 1777
Jno. Moore	London	(Pinchbeck)	c.1736
Jno. Myers	London	London 1774	1783–1804
Edw. Prideaux	London	London 1758	1743–90
Alex. Wilson	London	London 1775	1772–94
Thos. Worswick	Lancaster	Chester 1774	1753–1801
Crafts McKay	London	London 1781	1770–89
Ricd. Trap	London	London 1756	*ante* 1760
Rob. Green	Liverpool	London 1777	c.1767
Alex. Ainge	London	(Pinchbeck)	1749–83
Rob. Green	Liverpool	(Pinchbeck)	c.1767
Jno. Hilton	London	London 1786	? from 1698
Bouilon	Paris	——	? 1765
Rich. Barker	Liverpool	(Pinchbeck)	——
Ed. Fairclough	Liverpool	(Pinchbeck)	1774–1803
Barth. Davis	Preston	London 1763	*ante* 1762
John Bradfield	Liverpool	Birmingham 1796	? c.1816
Geo. Clark	London	None	1784–1804
Geo. Booth	Manchester	(Gilt)	1758–1788
John Page	Ipswich	(Gilt)	c.1740
Rich Burns.	Liverpool	London 1778	1790–1806
Arch. Coats	Wigan	Chester 1788	1767–97

Name	Address	Hallmark	Baillie/Britten
Uncased Movements			
John Bolton	Liverpool	——	1778
Jas. Walsh	Nantwich	——	——
Henry Perrier	London	——	c.1730
Thomason Fitter	London	——	1781–83
John Willis	London	——	——
Rob. Green	Liverpool	——	1767
Jas. Gray	London	——	ante 1760
Rich. Barnes	Birmingham	——	1781
Isaac Draper	London	——	1712
Rich. Ovingham	London	——	1776
James Stapely	Odiham	——	1757–95
Wm. Upjohn	Exeter	——	1741–75
Devereaux Bowlby	London	——	Died 1773
Charles Clay	London	——	1736
Ant. De Mayne	Woodbridge	——	1784
Thos Earnshaw	London	——	1745–1829

The outstanding feature of this list is that, with the exception of Rob. Green of Liverpool, each maker contributes only one movement. This underlines the fact that there were a relatively large number of watchmakers at work and that most (36 out of 40) appear in Baillie in this eighteenth-century period. It is, of course, impossible to go through Baillie's 36,000 entries line by line in order to find out the exact numbers over the whole century. For a very rough estimate I examined ten pages, taken at random through the book, and limited myself to those makers who could be calculated to be working during the twenty-five years from 1800 to 1825 when Baillie finished his entries. It would seem that there were over six thousand active watchmakers signing movements during this period. The geographical distribution was exactly the same as was found in my own randomly collected watches. So that 54 per cent of the makers were in or around London, as compared with 52 per cent in my collection. Baillie's figure for Liverpool makers was 11 per cent, whereas in my own collection with a Liverpool bias the figure was 20 per cent. Throughout the rest of the country makers were few and scattered. Of the larger cities, Manchester had 2 per cent, Birmingham 1 per cent and Bristol 1·5 per cent of the makers. Ireland managed to claim 6 per cent and Scotland did less well with only 3 per cent. Wales was impossible to assess by my sampling method because one was liable to find almost a whole page devoted to Jones, Evans, Roberts, Hughes, most of whom would be Welsh makers.

What the survey showed clearly was that London was predominantly the leading watchmaking centre and that its only challenger was Liverpool. This statement applies only, of course, to the finished and signed watch. As will be seen in a later chapter we are in the dark as to who made the *ébauche* or rough movement; they left no signature. Liverpool and surrounding towns would certainly be supplied from Prescot. Whether Clerkenwell made all the rough movements for the London finishers, or whether some or many also came from Lancashire, seems at present undetermined.

The neat, well-finished verge which characterized most of the eighteenth century presents as a high-water mark of English watchmaking. However, as far as the collector of today is concerned they will not be easily found and they will be expensive. In spite of the many watchmakers they would be relatively very expensive at the time that they were made. In the society of that day only the prosperous could afford to carry their own time with them. The majority had still to rely on public clocks and their striking. Present-day examples would, of course, be about two hundred years old and might have had a working life of something like a hundred years, during the course of which they may well have passed through the hands of jobbers and botchers as well as craftsmen repairers. Buying is therefore very much a gamble. Even if they are running this proves little more than the fact they are intact; excessive wear may be almost impossible to correct. It must be admitted that it was at this end of my collection that most of my buying errors were made. It is so easy to be charmed by the outward finish of a piece that is internally a repairer's nightmare. I was very fortunate to have the help of my friend, Mr. Robert Phillips, who was, after much reflection, able to salvage and restore nearly all my watches of this period.

11

The Early Eighteenth-century Verge

It has been noted that between, say, 1740 and 1800 the design of verges was fairly stable and characteristic—a small rounded outer case with an external hinge. This pattern was gradually coming into fashion, of course, before 1740 and the metal champlevé dial was disappearing in favour of the black-and-white enamel or porcelain dial. However, in the relatively short period, say, between 1690 and 1725 watches made in this country had a different and quite distinctive style. P. W. Cumhaill (*Investing in Clocks and Watches*, 1967) notes that with the adoption of the sprung balance the need for a stronger mainspring and the use of a decorated cock and footpiece resulted in a thicker watch. Some watches "*á l'anglais*" were produced with single cases, but the tendency was for pair cases, and the remainder, perhaps because they were wound through the dial retained the single case. They came to be known as "*oignons*" because of their high-domed glasses, which were fitted into the upper edges of an almost vertical bezel. It is very likely that they originally had protective cases, but these are rarely found. The classic dial for this type is of gilt metal but after the introduction of the concentric minute hand a further ring was added outside the chapter with small plaques for every fifth minute. Except for a few isolated examples the single case had died out in England and Holland by 1700 but the true pair case does not seem to have come into use immediately. Cumhaill mentions the frequency of repeater and alarm watches with pierced cases, sun and moon dials, and other elaborations.

These points were all confirmed by studying sixteen examples in the Liverpool City Museum—excluding the pierced cases which were of a somewhat earlier period. The sixteen watches all fell in the narrow period 1695 to 1725. Of these, twelve were presented with pair cases and four with only a single case. It was noted, however, that those where there was no outer case had pendant stems long enough to have allowed for this. Discounting the various elaborations, the basic dials were all similar. These were of metal, usually silver, with raised champlevé numerals for the hours while outside this chapter (but flush with the surface) were engraved rings containing the minute numerals. Hands were variations of the beetle-and-poker design. Glasses were of high camber, movements were deep and over all the watches were nearly round in outline, seen from the side view. In other words, the *oignon* or turnip shape. Makers' names were generally engraved on the dial. Two outstanding examples were one by Daniel Quare (hallmarked 1706-7) in gold with a repoussé case and one by Richard Vernon of Liverpool (1695-1700) in a silver case.

I became interested in this period after acquiring a simple but very good example (illustrations Nos. 78-81). It follows the above descriptions and examples closely. The silver case is single and large enough to make an outer case undesirable, and with a very deep glass the outline is very full indeed. There is no hallmark and here one may quote Britten: "Many early watch cases, especially silver ones of London make, are met with that have no hall-mark, the powers of the Company not being so strictly enforced then as now, or the value of the official assay not being so generally recognised." The casemaker's initials are of course stamped. On the dial, above and below the centre arbor, are engraved Cooper, London, The movement is engraved Edw. (or Edn.) Cooper, London. Baillie lists "Edward Cooper, London, early eighteenth century, watch Dennison collection". Britten (1932) lists "Edw. Cooper, London, watch, silver dial, raised figures, about 1730, conversion to rack lever and very large balance, about 1805". Possibly both are describing the same piece and both imply the absence of a more exact date, i.e., no hallmark. There is no date of Cooper's birth, no date of apprenticeship and no indication that he was a member of the Clockmakers' Company. The only clue to his existence, then, is this noted survival of one or possibly two watches. The long period of usage of my watch in single-case form is shown by the fact that the silver back of the case has actually worn through in two places. The case has been very cleverly patched from the inside by some later case repairer. Regulation is by Tompion rosette, the mainspring is set up by worm and screw, and the pillars are baluster. The movement is, of course, deep and heavy. The hands, beetle and poker, are rounded in section and probably cast rather than cut. The opening catch is inset into the numeral six. The glass is unscratched and the bezel sound. Mechanically the balance, the balance spring and mainspring, the fusee mechanism and chain are all intact and little worn, but there is considerable wear of the third wheel and pinion which will have to be renewed. On the whole, however, there is reasonable hope that the movement can be reinstated to something near its original condition. This has proved to be so.

12
The Rarer Escapements

For the practical collector this is nowadays very much a "never-never land". He can see these rarities in the museums, and though they can still be bought the cost is naturally very high. To possess such a piece, almost certainly in an expensive case, he will have to pay a sum which could be spent more interestingly on five or even ten more ordinary watches. It should also be remembered that it is very difficult to price a rare watch realistically and even more difficult to be sure that it is completely authentic. When the collector has gained experience and made his early mistakes he comes to see that to pay over the market price is a slur on his expertise. The field of rarer clocks and watches is one in which the amateur collector can mislead himself very easily. It is best left to the professional. My own contact has been confined to collecting examples (see illustrations Nos. 82–97) so that it would be foolish for me to write at length here, and in any case there is no need, for all the unusual escapements are covered lengthily in the standard books and coupled with much research on the history of the personalities involved. It is here that the literature runs into the obscure and the rare, and loses touch with the reality of holding a watch in one's hand and working out the lessons of its construction, or even more practically finding out what prevents it working. There are, of course, plenty of people who are quite happy with an armchair approach and of the many books perhaps that of Paul M. Chamberlain, *It's About Time*, is probably the most readable. However, if I seem unenthusiastic it is because the texts are so likely to let me down when seeking answers to simple everyday questions.

In a time of technical advance in horology all the watchmakers were, towards the end of the eighteenth century, seeking to improve on the verge. Everyone was inventing and patenting escapements, each adding a little more until the detached lever proved to be the final answer. In this experimental phase it would be quite impossible to illustrate all the various escapements. The most important in this country were the cylinder, the crank lever, the rack lever, the clubfoot or Ormskirk verge, and the duplex. Examples of all these occur in my collection and it is possible to say a few words about each. In general these were, and are in my example, watches within a date bracket of twenty-five years each side of 1800. Because of their rarity they are very likely to have been recased. One becomes plagued by this problem, and it is worth dealing with this in a separate chapter rather than at this stage: always bearing in mind that it will also arise when describing verges.

The Cylinder

Without going deeply into the history of the cylinder, which is usually attributed to George Graham (1675 to 1751), it is, particularly on the Continent, the most efficient and the most lasting competitor to the detached lever. However, as we have seen, the lever displaced it in this country from 1830 onwards. My examples consist of five cased and three uncased movements and cover a period (as far as they can be accurately dated) from 1785 to 1837.

The most authentic cylinder watch is one by Geo. Wilson which is case-dated London 1817. The only alteration is that of a replacement bow which in 18ct. gold could be expected to wear badly (the replacement was in 9ct. gold). The hands have also been replaced at some time. After being overhauled it keeps excellent time. The maker is not easy to trace and in the long list of Wilsons given by Baillie, George is a very rare Christian name. The George Wilson of the Strand died in 1774, but Britten notes a Geo. Wilson of Drury Lane with a single date of 1820, so we must assume him to be the maker. A second watch of an earlier date is engraved as being made by a better-known maker, William Seymour, who was a member of the Clockmakers' Company from 1766 to 1825 (Baillie). The case date is London 1785 and the case is, by presumption, of 22ct. gold, for it was not until 1798 that the 18ct. standard was re-introduced and the figures stamped. The whole watch looks completely original and authentic but it may have been recased. If so it has been fully restored to its original period. In mentioning these two watches and noting their attractiveness, it is perhaps unfortunate that they have to be kept in the bank.

The third cased cylinder fusee watch is by W & J Baird. This firm's dates are given as 1815 to 1825 by Baillie and from 1810 to 1830 by F. J. Britten—the latter probably being the more accurate. Almost certainly this firm was of high standing, for Baillie notes that there is a movement with detent escapement in the Ilbert Collection. In my example both the balance staff and the escape wheel are jewelled on ends though the cylinder is worn. However, on overhaul the timekeeping is very good. The case, silver pair, is suspect, being marked London 1837. The time lag is rather too long to be explained as chance, but if recased the result is an extremely good fit.

The fourth and fifth watches are insignificant pieces. One is an undated French movement and the other, by Sanders and Jacob of Dorchester (untraced), having a case date of 1882 London.

Three uncased cylinder escapements are good-class English examples. The first is by Barrauds of London who had their address in the Cornhill from 1798 onwards—the nearest designation to the vague "Barrauds" being Barraud & Sons, 1811 to 1835 (Baillie). The leading member of the family appears to have been Paul Phillip Barraud who was Master of the Clockmakers' Company in 1810 and 1811. The cylinder here is of steel and though not overhauled the movement is in full working order. The second movement is of eighteenth-century size with a steel cylinder and is complete and working. It is by Graham but not, almost certainly, the great George Graham. The christian name prefix is that of Jno., so presumably this is John who is given a single date of 1762 by Baillie. The piece is in fine condition with end jewels, dial regulator, uncracked dial, and square for setting up the spring. It is ticking away merrily and very quietly in front of me under its dust cover. The third movement is signed Jno. Willats of London and this is certainly the John Willats noted by Baillie as 1759, having died in 1762. The design is very similar to that of Graham though having square baluster pillars. It is intact but is not moving, probably due to wear of the steel cylinder. The hinge on the dial plate is broken and twisted, showing that the movement had been crudely wrenched out of the case by the hand of some bullion vandal. The pattern of the footplate to the cock is, like the cock itself, fully pierced for the design rather than simply engraved. This This was a common practice of the time shown by my more commonplace verge movements of the period.

The Rack Lever

This escapement was patented by Peter Litherland of Liverpool in 1791, Patent No. 1830 of 14 October, 1791, "Escapement to be applied to watches, clocks, or dials for use at sea or on land" (Aked, 1975). Historically speaking, the inspiration lay with Christian Huygens and the Abbé d'Hautefeuille about a hundred years earlier. Many watches on this principle were made by Litherland, his partners and successors, and quite a few found their way to America as part of the steady stream of finished watches that flowed out of the port of Liverpool. This was quite a step forward on the road to the fully detached lever, but Chamberlain maintains that it is a myth that the detached lever evolved from the rack by elimination of all but two teeth and giving a single tooth to the pinion. Though the simple rack-and-pinion conception was excellent, it still gave rise to friction and did not survive once the principle of complete detachment was achieved. All my examples are dated between 1800 and 1830; as we have seen previously, this latter date coincides with the blossoming of the lever. It should perhaps be noted that (as is seen in Chamberlain's illustration) the lever of the rack terminates at the outer end with a lunate or semi-circular counterpoise. It is this counterpoise that can be seen wagging away between the plates, and leads one to look for the less easily seen rack. A more cursory glance might lead one to think that the escapement was a simple detached lever.

In view of the importance of the Litherland family the information given by Baillie is helpful.

> Peter Litherland, 1790, died 1800. (He must have been working for many years before 1790.)
> Litherland, Whiteside and Co., 1800 to 1816. (Succeeded by Davies & Co.)
> Litherland, Davies and Co., 1818 to 1837.
> Richard Litherland, 1817 to 1829 (Liverpool).
> Ann Litherland, 1825 (Liverpool).

The various firms had premises in the centre of Liverpool—Mount Pleasant, Commutation Row, Church Street, Bold Street and Ranelagh Street—between 1796 and 1876 (Clutton and Daniels).

My best example of their work is a large pair-cased silver watch hallmarked Chester 1802 (see illustrations Nos. 86 and 87). The movement is engraved Litherland and Co., a titling that does not exactly fit any of the recorded styles of the firms. However, Baillie notes that there is a watch by Litherland and Co. (hallmark 1799) in the Ilbert Collection. The movement is numbered 2234. Peter Litherland took out a patent for this type of escapement in 1792 (No. 1889). According to Chamberlain the rack in such a plan carried thirty teeth and did away with the fourth wheel. The escape wheel made four revolutions a minute so that, most surprisingly, we see the second hand revolving completely every fifteen seconds. After overhaul the watch keeps very good time though some rather rough work had been previously done on it. There are also in my collection two additional movements, both very similar. The first, No. 3630, is engraved Litherland and Co., Liverpool, and winds through the dial. The balance wheel, which is of flat steel, is jewelled on the ends and in all there are eleven jewels in the movement. The foot of the cock is named by the word PATENT. Presumably the rack has only fifteen teeth, for there is no excessive swing of the balance wheel. The drive is by fusee. After overhaul the movement, which was in good condition, is working perfectly. The other movement is by Litherland, Whiteside and Co., Liverpool, No. 6692. It is not of quite such a high standard of workmanship as the former but, again, after overhaul it works well. The only other Litherland movement in the collection is one engraved Litherland Davies and Co., it carries the high number of 18177 and shows the classic Liverpool jewelling or Liverpool "windows". The number being much higher than the three earlier examples suggests a date at least in the 1830s and it is no surprise to find that the escapement is a detached lever. As with the rack levers, the word PATENT is still engraved on the balance cock.

Another maker of rack levers was Robert Roskell, also of Liverpool and comparably dated 1798 to 1830. Such a watch is a silver pair-cased example with the case in good repair and hallmarked London 1837 (see illustration No. 89). The hallmark is a little late, but Baillie notes that Robert Roskell worked in London as well as Liverpool, though he seems to have returned to Liverpool later and gone into business with his son. This rack lever does not beat seconds, though it is noted that he made such movements (Clutton and Daniels). After overhaul the watch is still working very well.

A third rack lever watch is an extremely good piece which again after overhaul continues to perform accurately. It is by William Lister of Newcastle upon Tyne (dated by Baillie, 1815 to 1820) and the case is hallmarked Chester 1815 (see illustration No. 90). Baillie also notes that Lister advertised chronometer watches, suggesting that he must have been a maker of repute; the family would seem to have been centred on Halifax. Whether Lister actually made the movement must be a matter of speculation. It is, of course, possible that it came in a finished state from Litherlands or even as a rough movement from, for instance, Prescot. Indeed, it would not surprise me if the majority of Litherland's movements were not built in the rough in nearby Prescot. The various addresses of the firm and its partnerships suggest retail shops in the best shopping streets in Liverpool, i.e., that the business was concerned with finishing watches rather than the whole process of manufacture. With this in mind I asked my watchmaker to take down the two Litherland movements again to look for evidence of the actual maker. There was, however, no specific mark or name to be found though this does not exclude the work having been put out from the main workshop to other specialists in the town. My feeling would still be that it would have needed a big organization to undertake the divisions of making, retail selling and repairing, and exporting.

The Clubfoot Verge

Though attributed to Peter Debaufre about 1704 this escapement was really only taken up in a practical way by the Lancashire watchmakers for a few years round about 1800. In fact it was alternatively known as the Ormskirk escapement. Its nickname of "the chaffcutter" is easily understandable when looking at the working watch. Having turned a hay chaffcutter for many hours in my youth, the two wheels revolving in opposite directions are very familiar. It was originally designed to retain the fusee and the contrate wheel; in other words, simply to replace the verge escapement. In an uncased movement by John Seed of Wavertree, Liverpool, this plan has been followed. This maker does not appear in Baillie but the number of the movement is 821. Engraved on the foot of the balance cock is the name Edward Woods but this does not give us any clue and the name may be that of the owner. The Ormskirk makers appear to have been more adventurous and, as has been noted earlier, they seem to have introduced the going barrel some sixty or eighty years before it came into general use in this country. In the movement that is functioning energetically in front of me at the moment there is a modern fully cased going barrel. Numbered 239 it was made by Joshua Rylands of Ormskirk whose date is given vaguely by Baillie as late eighteenth-century. Another Rylands, James Rylands of Ormskirk, whose death is recorded as 1803, has a clubfooted verge watch in the Science Museum, South Kensington.

My third example is by James Houghton of Ormskirk (see illustration No. 92). His dates are given by Baillie as 1800 to 1820. This movement has been recased rather obviously and despite overhaul it runs poorly. Power is taken from a spring without a fusee. The spring is held in place by a primitive barrel arrangement of four pins vertical to the pillar plate. Houghton is a very common Lancashire name. In *It's About Time* Chamberlain describes a clubfoot verge by Thos. Houghton (father of James), this time of Chorley, near Ormskirk. He says "This movement has no fusee and no barrel, the mainspring having its outer end attached to a pillar". The going barrel noted above in the movement by Joshua Rylands has the spring enclosed in a well-made modern barrel, though no doubt this could have been added at a later date. However, we see clearly in these descriptions the displacement of the fusee, perhaps for the first time in this country, at the beginning of the nineteenth century; whereas it would seem that the Prescot workers almost ignored the going barrel and continued with the fusee. Yet Ormskirk is only about fifteen miles from Prescot. Not that Prescot was alone in this lag; the country in general did not accept it till about 1880.

Like the rack lever, the clubfoot verge was ignored by the London makers. It flourished only round Ormskirk and was overtaken and put down by the lever. Neverthless it was in its day a stout workmanlike watch with a limited output as far as total numbers go.

The Duplex

The history and development of this escapement is set out in full detail in the standard horological texts and has been fully researched. There is, therefore, no immediate need for me to repeat what has often been said before. This was a precision escapement which flourished from about the middle of the eighteenth century to about 1850 both in France and this country. It was the domain of the leading London watchmakers and probably rarely made in the provinces. My few examples support this view. When made to the highest standards it was a precision movement made to last a hundred years, but not of such a high standard as the chronometer which overtook it. Both, of course, were supplanted by the detached lever. Britten, in writing of the duplex, goes into great detail to underline the very high degree of exactness needed in the setting up of the movement. He also notes the several points at which a good deal of wear occurs. His conclusion is: " . . . the idea of this escapement is seductive; at one time it was considered an ideal arrangement, but it has proved quite unreliable. The best proportion of its parts and the finest work are insufficient to prevent it 'setting'. On the introduction of the lever it declined and is rarely made now."

My first example is in a pair silver case, the movement number being 3360, and made by Thomas Earnshaw of London. One hopes that this is the first Thomas of lasting fame who is reported by Baillie as having repeater, cylinder, duplex, lever and chronometer watches in the Science Museum at South Kensington. Unfortunately it has not proved possible to find any list of movement numbers by which to check the date. When Thomas the first died in 1829 he was succeeded in his business in High Holborn by his son Thomas who died in 1850, and there was then yet another Thomas to carry on the business. The case is marked Birmingham 1797 and not, as one would expect, London. So this may have been a recasement, which such a high-class movement would have invited. If it is, then it has been extremely well done, looks completely original, and after overhaul keeps good time.

The second watch is engraved Grimalde and Johnson who, according to Britten's list, flourished at 431 The Strand, London, between 1815 and 1825. Peter Grimalde was in business on his own at the same address from 1800 to 1810 and is reported as a celebrated chronometer maker. The movement is again of a very high standard, the balance staff being jewelled on ends, and after overhaul it functions perfectly. Again, however, the hallmark on the pair silver case is out of step, being of Birmingham 1834. After all, one could reasonably suppose that, as in the Earnshaw example, two such high-grade movements started life in gold cases. Nevertheless the second marriage has been very harmonious, with precise fit, and has provided a much-enhanced setting to what would have been an interesting but homeless orphan.

The third duplex is also an uncased movement, a fusee duplex, No. 5435, by Barwise of London. John Barwise was a leading watchmaker, examples of his watches being preserved, together with his chronometers, in various collections. He was also the chairman of the ill-fated British Watch Company which was in 1843 strangled at birth by the Parliamentary opposition of the watchmaking trade. He was in business at 29 St. Martin's Lane, London, from 1790 to 1842.

Again we have the same high-class workmanship, though only the balance staff and the escape wheel are jewelled. The balance wheel is rather unusually heavy, of square sectioned brass, but the regulator is mounted in modern style on the balance cock. It is probably dated about 1830 and though rather sluggish in action without an overhaul it is still working. The hinge plate has been completely wrenched away by the man who separated it from its original gold case.

There is an interesting comment on Barwise arising from that remarkable book, *The Reminiscences and Recollections of Captain Gronow* (Bodley Head, 1964). Just before Waterloo, Gronow found himself stationed with his regiment of the Guards in London and likely to miss the engagement. He therefore obtained attachment to join the staff of Sir Thomas Picton and embarked for Brussels, arriving on the field on the eve of Waterloo. He was immediately sent to take charge of French prisoners held at Quatre Bras. At daylight on the 18th of June he was relieved by a detachment of the 3rd Guards, among whom was Ensign George Anson. "I took the opportunity of giving Anson, then a fine lad of seventeen, a silver watch, made by Barwise, which his mother, Lady Anson, had requested me to take over to him." Anson survived Waterloo and later became a distinguished General. In view of the silver casing it might be surmised that this was not one of Barwise's most distinguished watches such as a cylinder—no doubt it was a simple verge. The story emphasizes the calls that wars always make upon the supply of watches and the Napoleonic period was no exception. Napoleon himself, it was thought, was a demanding client of Breguet. Captain Gronow goes on to add, apropos Breguet: "This celebrated man was greatly encouraged by the Allies (when they entered Paris) in 1815. The Emperor Alexander purchased several of his watches and the Duke of Wellington also had one which, on touching a spring at any time, struck the hour and the minute . . . . it cost, I am told, three hundred guineas. I frequently visited his shop and had many conversations with him, and, though he was at that time getting old, he was full of energy and vivacity."

The Chronometer Escapement

Though this is the ultimate in precision for the traditional watch, it is extremely costly to build and while in use needs to be carefully protected. Nevertheless pocket watches with this escapement were built throughout the nineteenth century. They were only made by top-class tradesmen and they are described in detail and with historical notes in all the books. Despite this wealth of attention, my own experience would strongly suggest that very few such watches were in fact made, in comparison with the detached lever. My collection cannot boast even an uncased movement, mainly, no doubt, because even the most hard-hearted bullion man would realize that an intact chronometer watch would always be worth more than the gold in the case. This has always been so, with the result that such a watch would command a high price.

Other less-known Escapements

Such was the urge to improve, that in addition to the rarer escapements described here there are many others even less known still. These are best explored in the book *It's About Time* by Paul M. Chamberlain. In general terms, however, the commoner variants are noted in the chapter on the "Evolution of Watch Escapements" and the more abstruse in the chapter on the "Development of Watch Escapements".

A final note might be added here on an escapement that might be regarded as rare and abstruse by the ordinary collector, namely the Massey or crank lever escapement. Mr. Alan Treherne has been particularly interested in this subject to which an introduction is given in the catalogue of an exhibition at the Newcastle-under-Lyme Museum (1977) on the Massey Family. Here are to be found diagrams of the five types of escapement together with watches made by the Masseys, and perhaps more importantly watches by other makers in which the escapement was used—with or without acknowledgement. My own interest was initially confined to a single example, an uncased movement by Jas. Cornwall of Liverpool (No. 782). More recently I was lucky enough to pick up an intact and working watch by F. J. (Francis Joseph) Massey of 17 Chadwell St., Clerkenwell. His dates are given as 1839 to 1844. The movement number is 6088 and the London hallmark is 1839. After overhaul there is reasonable timekeeping and a most energetic action. (See Illustration No. 99). Shortly after a good silver hunter came along in full working order. It was by Robt. Roskell of Liverpool (No. 39740) and hallmarked Chester 1826. Alan Treherne immediately showed me that it was a Massey escapement without any acknowledgement to Massey. To me it had passed as an ordinary fusee lever. Spurred by this I then examined all the uncased "fusee lever" movements in my collection. The balance cock was removed and the type of roller carefully inspected. No fewer than six more Massey escapements were uncovered. One was by Robt Roskell (No. 38737), one by Jas. Hornby, Liverpool, one by Frodsham? Liverpool, one by Ezechial Mason, Liverpool, one by W. Hamlet, Liverpool, and the last anonymous. Four movements had Liverpool jewelling.

The story of these "discoveries" defies comment. It shows that crank lever escapements lurk undetected and that the Massey family, predominantly escapement makers, supplied many other makers who often did not specifically engrave an attribution of the various Massey patents. Furthermore, as Alan Treherne maintains, Edward Massey played a very important part in the work that lead up to the final development of the fully detached lever.

13
Leverization

HAVING illustrated the story of the verge by reference to commonplace examples and the supplanting of this escapement by the detached lever, the collector should be prepared to realize that the transition could be carried out by planned surgery. As the verge and other escapements became worn out or damaged they could be replaced by the new-fangled lever, just as the verge escapement of a clock was often converted to an anchor. In a full turn of the wheel it is now fashionable to convert them back to the original arrangement. In the case of watches the term "leverization" was used. Though this must have been quite a common treatment for the elderly watch whose owner was reluctant to part with it, there is almost no reference to it in the texts. Indeed the only reference I have been able to find is the following short note by Eric Bruton in his *Clocks and Watches, 1400 to 1900:* "A large number of English watches of the early nineteenth-century were converted to lever escapement from duplex or perhaps cylinder, so what appears an early lever watch should always be regarded with suspicion until proved to be so." Britten's *The Watch and Clockmakers' Handbook, Dictionary and Guide* was first published in 1884 but by 1896 it was in its ninth edition. Under the heading of "Conversion" he gives a full account which includes details of how the new trainwork can be calculated and substituted.

Many watches were leverized very expertly with happy results. It is by no means easy to detect that the operation has been carried out though, of course, case dates and makers' names will suggest this. According to Clutton and Daniels, "it is probably true to say that no more than two dozen English lever escapement watches survive from before 1800 ... after this (time), no more is heard of the escapement in England for 15 years". In other words, any lever escapement appearing in a watch dated before 1815 is almost certainly a verge replacement. Such substitution is, of course, perfectly legitimate and above criticism so long as nobody is misled.

There are two examples in my collection. The first is a watch by Alexande Ainge of London who, according to Baillie, was apprenticed in 1749 and was a member of the Clockmakers' Company from 1766 to 1783. The case, which is typical eighteenth-century in style, is pinchbeck (therefore lacking any hallmark) and has an outer covering of tortoiseshell. The movement has been expertly leverized and after overhaul functions well. It is abundantly clear that this watch could only have been made as a verge in the first place. The second is an uncased movement of characteristic eighteenth-century verge type with the hinge broken as it was wrenched out of the original gold case. Winding is through the dial as well as through the dust cover at the back. Regulation is provided by an arbor square and the traditional steel dial visible through the dust cover. The balance cock is round and the balance staff jewelled on ends. In other words, we have an easily recognizable eighteenth-century verge movement. It is numbered 3813 and signed Thos. Earnshaw, London. As the first and celebrated Thomas Earnshaw died in 1829 at the age of eighty, it is reasonable to assume that he made the watch as a verge before 1800. However, since I have no lists of movement numbers there may be holes in this reasoning. Moreover, Clutton and Daniels note that Earnshaw "was perhaps the first leading maker to make quite cheap, single roller, lever escapement watches in the last year or two of his life". In this instance the lever escapement is mounted on a bridge screwed to the pillar plate and to my amateur eye there are no other clues to the existence of the previous verge escapement. The movement appears to be quite intact.

I asked Mr. Phillips to overhaul the movement and he reports as follows:

Pivot holes in the frames are there to confirm that Movement No. 3813 by Earnshaw was in its early life a verge escapement. Other holes have been plugged with brass, finished off and then re-gilded. To complete the conversion, two detachable bridges were made to carry the altered train. One pillar plate (dial side) and the other inside the dial plate. The dial side bridge was drilled to accommodate the new third wheel, which engaged the centre wheel. The fourth pinion seems to be original. This engages the new escape wheel (rachet type) whose pivot holes are jewelled, recessed in the bridge, and held in position with screws. This wheel engages the new pair of pallets (which are jewelled) and hence to the new balance wheel. This has no appearance of being the original except for the jewel hole and end cap jewel of the balance bridge. The fusee chain is original, but I suspect that the mainspring has been changed to a weaker one as compared to the strength of a mainspring usually found in verge movements. The method of hooking the mainspring is that of a stud fitting, which at that period was the English method. The great disadvantage of the conversion is that the fusee had not been designed to have maintaining power (the "Going Fusee" invented by John Harrison 1750). This means that when winding the movement, power is taken off the going train and so stops the vibrations of the balance which (may be 16,200). The condition of the movement is very good, hardly any wear to the teeth of the fusee or centre pinion. The conversion has resulted in nine jewels—i.e., 'scape pivot holes, pallets, table roller, upper and lower balance holes and end cap jewels. The motion work is original but regret that I don't know how the train work was calculated to use the original motion work. Condition of lower balance pivot poor due to short pivot on staff which is slightly out of upright. The under side of the balance has been filed either for poising or to reduce weight.

Subsequently I came across another leverized verge among my uncased movements. This was engraved Chisholm and Co., Charing Cross, London, No. 656. It was index regulated, fusee driven, with seconds dial and modern hands. It must have been a mid-nineteenth-century movement as the back plate had no decoration at all nor had the cock. The head of the cock was simply a round brass plate covering the balance wheel completely. The leverization was essentially by means of the bridges as in the Earnshaw movement. It struck me that this particular movement might have been the result of the maker using his old stock of half-made-up verges (when these became unfashionable) to produce a hybrid from the beginning of the movement's life.

Clearly verges were not ideally suited for leverization, but this would have been the best solution, after levers became available, for the worn-out verge with an erratic rate. Other escapements were also converted as the lever swept into popularity—many, no doubt, because of the simple advantage in time-keeping or because of the difficulty of making major repairs to complicated movements. In order to simplify the procedure I am told that the firm of Rotherham and Sons made special "kits" for this purpose which could be reasonably easily fitted by the watchmaker. The detent of the chronometer is fragile and the owner might well have settled for leverization as much cheaper, as a broken cylinder needed a highly skilled piece of repair work. This might have been bypassed in the same way, which could well apply to rack lever, duplex, clubfoot verge and other obsolete escapements. Another reason for leverization was a noisy movement, the prime offender in this disturber of sleep being the clubfoot verge.

It is likely that leverization flourished in the middle years of the last century and has now been forgotten. It should be noted that it is not always easy to be sure what the original escapement was before the alteration.

14
Regulation

It is not always possible in the restoration of an old watch to ensure that "it is under the power of the regulator". Usually this is because the balance spring has become shortened by losing pieces of the outer coil in the passage of time. These have broken off at the point where the spring is pinned into the cock. These earlier springs were, naturally, dubious affairs with few turns and of a material far different from the sophisticated modern hairspring. In a high-class well-adjusted, modern watch the coil swells and pulsates with the utmost smoothness, and can be seen to do so because it is mounted above the balance wheel. Shortly after 1661 Tompion began to use variation of the effective length of the spring to control the rate. If the spring was lengthened the movement ran more slowly; if shortened then the rate was faster. It was so simple and so fundamental that this method of regulation—and no other—has been in use ever since in all spring-driven watches. However well read we may be, it is almost impossible for us to conceive what life was really like three hundred years ago and yet most of us still carry round every day a relic of those times—the lever escapement.

Tompion's simple idea was to place two close-set curb pins one each side of the terminal coil of the balance spring. At the point at which they impinged the vibration of the spring was damped down and its effective length determined. The curb pins were moved along the terminal coil by means of a simple arc and wheel. The index was the "figure plate" or "rosette" to be found on the top plate of most seventeenth- and all eighteenth-century verges. This was arbitrarily numbered 0 to 5 or 0 to 6, and occasionally the index finger of an engraved hand pointed to the number in use. More usually, however, the position engaged was a matter of some guesswork, The rosette was turned by a square on the arbor and this square might well be of a different size to the winding square. When the rosette was turned clockwise the rate was advanced and vice versa. Tompion's regulator, as shown by my watches and noted in the texts, was universally used until about 1800, when it rather suddenly succumbed to that of Bosley on the grounds of simplicity. In the transitional phase the obsolete rosette was replaced by a blank blued disc, which can be seen in the illustrations looking like a piece of decoration.

The successor to Tompion's regulator was patented as early as 1755: "Bosley, Joseph, No. 698. 1.4.1755—a new movement in watches; also slide for regulating watches". The delay in its introduction was considerable, but since it had advantages over that of Tompion, it at last became popular by 1800. None of my eighteenth-century verges shows its use, but by 1830 it was the universal verge regulator and continued so as long as verges were made. Two of my watches case-dated 1910 and 1912, are the most modern English-made watches in which it appears, so Bosley had a long run. Camerer Cuss, in *The Country Life Book of Watches*, gives this description: "In 1755 Joseph Bosley patented 'A newly invented slide, which slide has no wheel attached to it'; that is, he dispensed with the Tompion rack. Bosley's consisted of a small lever, the shorter end of which carried the curb pins which embrace the balance spring, the longer end (by which it is moved) travels across the scale which serves to indicate the alteration to 'fast' and 'slow' in the position of the curb pins." The scale was engraved on the top plate so that at last the owner could regulate his own watch in a simple manner. All this is clearly shown in my pieces of this period where the spring was still retained in a position under the balance. Also clearly shown is a modification of Bosley used after the spring had migrated under the cock. Here the index was clipped round the endstone in the modern manner. But instead of the index arm lying on the top of the cock it pointed in exactly the opposite direction as a continuation of the cock. It then cranked downwards outside the balance wheel and registered in the old way on an arc engraved on the top plate. In these cases the spring was always pinned to a corresponding arm rising from the top plate and coming over or under the balance wheel.

On the whole, the horological texts do not go into much detail about regulation and regulators but it seems to me that the collector should be aware of the varying phases. The best account is by Chamberlain in his paper on "Watch Regulators" in *It's About Time*. However, much of the information relates to the modern watch and the refinements of the index which provided micrometer adjustment without backlash. Such regulators are frequently shown by the more modern part of my collection and there is no need to repeat Chamberlain's excellent account. There is, however, one short throw-away sentence which seems to me to be of great importance since the point appears not to be made elsewhere: "This [regulator] was used in connection with the balance spring put under the balance wheel." The spring can be placed above or below the wheel without affecting the efficiency of the balance one way or another. The point to be made is that in the early watches up to, say, 1830 the spring was always under the wheel, between it and the top plate: with the result that Tompion's regulator, and later Bosley's, were both fixed to the top plate and acted from below. By the end of the nineteenth century most of the balance springs had migrated to a position between the cock and the wheel and regulation was consequently from above. I have not been able to discover the reason for this change in position. There may be a technical reason, but it may simply have been a wish to bring the spring out of its hiding place for better access and inspection.

To illustrate the apparent confusion I examined my nine examples of silver-cased going barrel levers. Three had a straight index on the cock with the spring above the balance wheel. Two had the spring uppermost and had a modified Bosley regulator. In the remaining four the spring was still in its old position under the balance with traditional Bosley regulation. These watches all fell into the period between 1891 and 1916. The latest to retain the spring under the wheel was dated 1911. In examining twelve undated and uncased movements with a full-plate going barrel layout there were two with a modern index, two with a modified Bosley and eight with a traditional Bosley regulator. Adding the figures together we see:

     Modern index   5 examples
     Modified Bosley 4 examples
     Traditional Bosley 12 examples

As far as fusee levers (from 1830 onwards) were concerned, the lower position of the balance spring was overwhelmingly favoured. Taking my series of thirty-five uncased, and therefore undated, movements first: twenty-nine of these favoured the lower position of the spring; of the remaining six, three had an ordinary index and three had a modified Bosley regulator. The twenty-six cased watches could be dated, of course, by the hallmark, the earliest being 1833 and the latest 1910. Of these, twenty had the spring in the lower position with Bosley regulation. Four others had the spring uppermost and used the modified Bosley. Only two showed the modern index, one being dated 1896. The other was most surprising, for it was case-dated 1834, being one of the earliest detached levers in the collection. The maker was Rich. Thelwell of Manchester and the hallmark Chester. It was a well-made watch with a sprung dust cover and apparently all original. It was fitted with a balance spring above the wheel and a modern index which appeared to be original. Otherwise the earliest appearance of the modern index in my fusee levers was in 1896.

The Bosley regulator appears to have held the field throughout the fusee lever period. When we look at the over-all position of sixty-one watches and escapements the division is as follows:

Modern index	5 examples
Modified Bosley	7 examples
Traditional Bosley	49 examples, or 80 per cent

It has not been possible to trace any inventor's name for what has been called here the modified Bosley regulator or indeed for the inventor of the straight modern index, though there are, of course, many named variations of the latter.

Within the period 1880 to about 1900 we have the three-quarter-plate keyless English lever, the three-quarter-plate keyless chronograph, and the three-quarter-plate fusee keywind chronograph. Examination of a series of twenty-four of the movements showed that in all the balance spring was mounted in the upper position and all were regulated by the straight modern index. This shows that the English makers were thoroughly conversant with this regulation but only consistently used it in the three-quarter-plate movements. No doubt this was because the layout left them with no other choice. Beyond this the evidence suggests that, unless he was forced to do otherwise, the English maker preferred the older position of the balance spring and the older method of regulation.

It was, of course, otherwise with the American and Swiss makers who regularly used the index on the cock, and certainly all the imported watches showed this. It seems likely that the Bosley regulator was little, if ever, used abroad and that the most favoured position of the balance spring was above the balance from, say, 1850. As Chamberlain notes, one of the earliest patents was for the whiplash regulator first introduced by Reed in 1865, and all the many variations subsequently used were based on the simple index carried on the cock. These were all micrometer adjustments to the index finger but, as Chamberlain also notes, if friction of the mounting is done away with then the simple straight index is quite good enough for regulation.

Chamberlain also mentions the free-sprung watch, i.e., one in which no regulator is used. Here adjustment was done by removing the balance and altering the setting of timing screws. This would only be used in high-grade and chronometer movements. Watches without an index must be very rare and in order to carry the set rate continuously must be of very high standard. Only one such watch occurs in my collection. This is a chronograph by John Kellie of Norton Street, Liverpool. It is in an 18ct. gold case, heavily made and hall-marked Chester 1900. Kellie had a very good reputation. He may have built the movement in his own workshop or alternatively had it made by the Lancashire Watch Company of Prescot. The movement was overhauled by my friend Stanley Smith who set it with a gain of five seconds a day, using his timing machine for this purpose, of course. This unusual movement is mentioned only to emphasize that a watch without means of day-to-day regulation is hardly a practical proposition.

15

Pocket Watch Cases

THE academic horologist might well feel that once the movement and escapement of a watch have been discussed, there is little more to add. For the collector, however (and even more so for the owner), the case is very important—it is the watch's public image, the bearer of the impression made upon those who view it. Without a case the movement cannot function as a watch and must lie idle.

Casemakers were a quite separate discipline among the many divisions of watchmaking, and there were three approaches to casemaking: the individual casemaker; the casemaker working to instructions from the maker/finisher; and the small factories.

Throughout the pocket watch era there was always the individual casemaker who was a master craftsman, supervising a small workshop with crude tools and primitive power. Such a workshop, that of one of the last surviving London casemakers, a Mr. Oliver, has been preserved and set up in the Liverpool City Museum. The work of these craftsmen is identified by his personal initials punched on the case. He would receive a finished movement and case it according to the instructions given to the maker/finisher by the customer. Alternatively the finisher, having bought the movement would instruct the casemaker and sell the finished article. There would be little in the way of standardization, except perhaps in very small batches, and each case was a tailor-made "one-off" job. When the small factories of Coventry and Birmingham were better organized, larger batches and runs of standardized sizes were possible and the makers could offer the retailers the finished watch, using a catalogue. Either the maker's name or the retailer's name would be engraved, or the watch could remain anonymous. My watches suggest that Clerkenwell did quite a lot of business on these lines with a case hallmark of London. In America and later in Switzerland the third approach of casemaking developed: that of mechanized factories turning out standardized cases to fit standardized factory-made movements.

The outcome of these three different approaches to casemaking was exactly the same as the outcome of the development of the machine-made movement, and oddly enough, it was the same man, Aaron L. Dennison, who accomplished it. (His middle name was Lufkin or Lupkin.) He succeeded in making the initials A.L.D. as well known in casemaking as the A.W.W. company was in movements. Dennison had eventually given up trying to make watches, and had decided to specialize in the simpler field of cases and establish something "that would support him in his old age". In 1870 he came to Handsworth, near Birmingham, where he concentrated on the problem of mechanizing the trade of casemaking, with such success that, in association with Alfred Wigley, he was able to compete successfully with similar firms, both in America and Switzerland, and capture virtually the whole of the English market. Dennison was the active head of the firm until his death at the age of 83 in 1895. The firm was carried on by one of his sons, but it did not successfully cater for the wrist watch trade in the same way that it had monopolized the pocket watch trade. The firm of Benson Bros. (B.B.) of Wood Street, Liverpool, made many cases for the Lancashire trade, but with the decline of the pocket watch it was absorbed into the Dennison Watchcase Company, and both disappeared, I understand, in the 1960s.

Some American and Swiss watches were imported complete but the majority arrived as movements only, to be cased and hallmarked in Birmingham. My collection confirms the Dennison Watchcase Company's domination of the English scene in the closing phases of the pocket watch.

The size of the finished case deepened on the size of the movement. In the usual Lancashire range this covered twenty sizes from 1·2 inches to 2·0 inches. Movements were traditionally measured in external diameter in an obscure and antique French measure of *lignes*. Most twentieth-century gentleman's watches were fairly uniform at a diameter of about 2 inches. The dress watch was smaller and the chronograph and other more massive cases went up to possibly $2\frac{1}{2}$ inches.

The whole success of casemaking depends on how effectively dust and moisture can be excluded. The difficulty is that two-thirds of the volume of the case is occupied by air, which when heated in the pocket to body temperature expands and leaks out. When it cools down, for instance on the dressing table at night, air is sucked in and brings with it a variable amount of dust and damp which mounts up as time passes. Waterproofing is too recent a development to apply to the pocket watch. The waistcoat pocket is, in general, nothing more than a dust trap. Knowing this, the careful owner would carry his watch in a chamois leather slip-on bag. These can still be bought and add the finishing touch to a prize specimen.

Looking at the traditional case in detail, we can see its dust and moisture weaknesses. The factory-made case would be more likely to reach a higher standard of machining than the hand-made case. If the bezel is hinged, wear in the hinge will lead to poor seating. A snap-on is better, at least in an open-faced type; in hunter cases there are potential gaps both at the top and the bottom of the bezel. We can hope that the flat or lunette glass will fit close and well into the bezel grove. The main central part of the case—the body—should be unjointed with integral stem, but this leaves access under the winding button and down the sleeve. The hinge interferes with effectiveness of the case back. Snap-on backs are unusual, but the screw-back has been used to give a closer fit. These can be detected by the milled edge (to give a grip to the fingers) and the number of disfiguring scratches where attempts have been made to open with a knife blade. The recommended method of opening is to get a screwing grip by placing the watch between the palms of the hands. Closure is rarely easy because the entering threads of the screws are often damaged in the course of time. The final protection is given by the dome. This is only rarely omitted from a case and then only to save cost in a gold case. Both back and dome are lipped for opening, always at the one o'clock position.

It is interesting to see the expert opening and closing a pocket watch—something that might seem very simple to most people. Cases are not designed to be opened by the thumb nail, which is often too thick to enter the outside lip and unlikely to overcome the snap of the inner lip if this is a good one and the back is as tight-fitting as it should be. However, the nail is unlikely to gouge or scar the case as it slips in the way that a knife will. Such scratches, which are difficult to buff off, should leave a mental scar on the collector, particularly if he makes one himself. The expert uses a specially made watch-opening knife with a blunted point and rounded edges (see illustration No. 119). These can still be bought and every collector should have one. The sure hand of the tradesman watch repairer always relies on his pocket knife—but then he never scratches a case. In closing the case, and before handing it back to the customer, the finger- and thumb-marks on the dome and the back are cleaned off with chamois leather. In more authoritarian days the assistant who couldn't give a watch back to his client properly was liable to be given a reprimand, if not the sack, just as was the repairer who allowed his screwdriver to slip and scratch the plate or burr the slot of the screw head.

With the advent of the fusee lever in this country my watches show an immediate slimming which, of course, the horizontal layout of the escapement made possible. In my large series of these watches none shows a pair case, though these were still in favour for the verges still being made. It was only recently that I saw, but did not buy because of the unrealistically high price, a gold pair-cased fusee lever, case-dated 1843. There will, of course, be others somewhere but, based on my personal experience, they must be very rare indeed. The fusee silver-cased lever was, in the middle fifty years of the last century, the most elegant of watches ever made in this country. Such plain good design was usually the prerequisite of the best French makers, from whom it was no doubt copied. There was no obtrusive winding button, the bezel was narrow, the numerals slim and tall, the seconds dial flush and the seconds hand shaped. There was no attempt at any decoration and the maker did not write on the dial. The only drawback was that occasionally the whiteness of the dial tended to cream with age just as a clock dial does. Perhaps, like the clock dial, it was only painted and not fired. On looking through my fusee movements it was the later ones, i.e., with a sunk seconds dial and thick and well-fired enamel, that retained their whiteness. Those with a flush seconds dial had a thinner, more matt, finish and had become creamy white. The dialmakers would seem to have altered and improved their methods later to get a permanent brilliant white shade. When the mid-century fusee levers were gold cased and plain they were, of course, equally attractive. It is, however, usual to find them with a fussily decorated gold dial more attractive as a piece of jewellery, and much the same can be said for the silver cases with silver dials. Towards the last quarter of the nineteenth century the slim elegance of the case was lost and the later Victorians favoured large, heavy, thick cases with thick ungainly numerals.

Most of my pair-cased verges in both the eighteenth and nineteenth centuries are with few exceptions silver cased. The reasoning behind this is, in my opinion, far more interesting to the collector to spend his money on a variety of movements, by different makers, than to invest it in a few gold cases. For the investor, of course, the position is reversed. He should buy good names in magnificent gold cases. The general design, both of the smaller eighteenth-century and the larger nineteenth-century case, has already been described. Apart from the size, the main distinguishing dating feature is the hinge (and to a lesser extent the shape of the bow). There are no examples in the collection of the square-cornered outside hinge to the outer case—in earlier examples the hinges were even given an acute angle. Both were liable to catch in the pocket lining. At least by 1725 the corners were smoothed or chamfered off (this is shown in my earliest watch) and the hinge is preparing to retreat into the general outline of the case, as it did about 1800. It has remained there ever since, at first with the hinge pin still obvious and, later still, almost invisible.

After the many years of use that our pieces have had there are several places to look to for excessive wear which will impair the appearance and value. The bow and its pin are often thin and show much play in the stem. The glass is often worn and scratched. This gives a blurred and dirty appearance to the dial and unfortunately cannot be remedied as in the modern watch by having a new glass fitted, since new glasses are not generally obtainable. Possibly the glass could be repolished or even less likely there may be someone who could make a new one. The point to be made here is that a collector would be unwise to buy a piece with a cracked or blurred glass. On the other hand, he should never pass by the chance of buying old pocket watch glasses, of whatever age, such as might occur when an old watch-repairing business is wound up. One of my friends in the trade sold me a small number of unused verge glasses which he had come across in an old bureau.

Liverpool's last independent casemaker died some thirty years ago. His successor was only a case repairer; he too has now gone, but in his time he refurbished quite a few of my damaged and worn cases. It is now difficult to find a case repairer, though this can be done by enquiries through the trade.

Case Materials

The collector should know the type of metals used in a case and go into this in detail, for in establishing the provenance of the watch the case is at least as important as the evidence provided by the movement. One can find cases which now hold a movement that is not the original and of course vice versa. This will be discussed in chapter 19. Predominantly, the metals used were gold and silver, platinum being rarely found. Brass is almost never found in its crude state. Iron and steel were of little use because of rusting, and stainless steel, the metal of choice today, was not available when pocket watches were in general use. Gunmetal cases are cheap and satisfactory but unattractive and are to be found in army-issue watches which often had good or high-class movements. We are left then with the consideration of gold, silver and rolled gold.

From A.D. 1300 all gold articles in this country had by law to be assayed for their gold content and stamped in the various assay offices scattered throughout the country. Imported cases were also supposed to be assayed and marked as foreign but for some years it would seem that the assay of the country of origin has been accepted—e.g., 14K on a Swiss watch case. In contrast, gold coins and gold medallions—all 22-carat—when issued by the Mint have no assay mark. The collector will be well served by the booklet *Bradbury's Book of Hallmarks* used by the jewellery trade and usually on sale in such shops. He will rarely need the expensive tomes dependent on research carried back for centuries to areas where doubts might arise.

What has to be remembered is that before 1798 cases were made of 22-carat gold and carried no carat mark. After this date the 18-carat standard was introduced (as 22-carat was a soft and easily worn material) and both grades were clearly marked in numbers. The 22-carat gold still carried (until 1844) the lion passant mark, while the 18-carat case was given a crown, which subsequently became the universal mark of all standards of gold. In this country we have long discarded the 15, 14 and 12-carat standards and use as an alternative to 18 only the 9-carat—marked 9ct. and ·375.

The simple explanation of carat values is that 22-carat gold is compounded of twenty-two parts of gold and two parts of alloy; the 18-carat gold contains eighteen parts of gold and six parts of alloy; and so on down the scale. Various metals are used as alloys and by manipulation give different tints from white gold to red gold or even more exotic shades, for example, green gold. In sovereigns it is possible that the shade was also determined by supplies from different mining areas—Ashanti gold is, for instance, a very red colour. When thinking of bullion values it will, of course, be realized that pure or fine gold has a 24-carat standard and the world price of this standard is carried daily by the *Financial Times* and *The Daily Telegraph* in dollars per ounce fine. Thus the value of an 18-carat case is only three-quarters of this quoted price, and of 9-carat only half of that again. Difficulties can be resolved by speaking to a bullion dealer who keeps in touch with the opening, interim and closing prices on the Exchange. He will tell you the selling price in pounds of the two carat values and his buying price for gold scrap—which is naturally lower.

It is, incidentally, not easy to find the exact weight of a gold case. For this you need an experienced jeweller or repairer. He has to remove the movement, of course, and then the glass from the bezel. In hunter watches and those with flap backs it is necessary to extract the springs which curve inside the body of the case. Finally, the winding button (which is usually gilt brass) and the sleeve are removed. The stripped case can then be weighed on a troy weight spring balance or more exactly on jeweller's scales. Having done this the craftsman must have the skill to reassemble the case. In practice the case is simply weighed without the movement and an allowance made for the *in situ* extras.

The asking price of a gold-cased watch must largely be influenced by the caseweight factor. The amateur should be on his guard against the dealer's easy assumption that "there must be at least so much worth of gold in the case itself". It is true that I have, in more favourable times, bought watches in which the scrap value of the case was indeed up to the level of the dealer's estimate or possibly more than the price put on the whole watch, but the buyer needs to do some careful pencil-and-paper homework to see where he stands. In any case as a collector he is buying a watch as a complete entity, not for the purpose of destroying it to make a small profit. There is a very important guideline, which applies to all collecting but is highlighted by the intrinsic expense of the gold case. The collector must have enough expertise in his subject not only to know the technical value and standing of the piece but also its proper market price—this needs to be underlined heavily. Those who carry the bidding well beyond the point at which the dealers drop out are backing their own taste but showing no expertise. Of course, we all hope that our special knowledge will bring up hidden treasures and so it may well do.

If I seem to labour this question of bullion value it is because it is so important in deciding what a collector can buy, and quite divorced from the real collecting interest which lies in the period, the maker, the type of movement, and its history and rarity. Other factors forcing up the price and limiting his choice are inflation, investment buying, the drain abroad (particularly to America), and the natural and growing scarcity of the older pieces. The antique (i.e., made before 1830) is a field largely barred to him, although until recently excluded from Value Added Tax. It is for this reason that this book, though based on my collection reaching back to the eighteenth century, pays particular attention to Victorian and Edwardian watches. It is agonizing for today's collector to look back to the days when the going price of the ordinary silver verge was round the five-pound mark and there were plenty of them. To be fair, however, it must be remembered that today's prices only mirror today's apparent affluence. At the time when prices were seemingly low the collector would have had very few spare five-pound notes to take advantage of them.

At this point we should note the gilt case. Brass case verges were gilded to produce a low-priced watch which superficially looked like gold but, of course, carried no assay mark—only the initials of the casemaker. The process used was the highly dangerous mercury-gilding which has long been illegal in this country. Today we would use electroplating with a gold electrode which would be weighed before and after use to determine the weight of gold used. Any required thickness can be deposited and there is a wide range of colour in the tinting of gold. In practice, however, electroplating was rarely if ever used for pocket watch cases. It wears through as did the old-fashioned gilding. For this reason eighteenth-century verges were often gilded on the inside and outside of the inner case and the inside of the outer case. The outer case, where the wear occurred, was best given a shagreen cover. This could be real sharkskin (and there are basking sharks off the coasts of this country) or more ordinary leather worked up to pass as real shagreen. Pinchbeck, invented about 1725 according to Britten, is sometimes found as a finish but it is not clear how this can be distinguished from ordinary gilding. The composition of this material is given as four parts of copper to three of zinc. How the formula was compounded seems, however, to be a family secret which is said to have been lost after the death of Edward Pinchbeck, who succeeded to the business of his father Christopher Pinchbeck, the inventor. The best account of the Pinchbeck era can be found in Britten's *Former Clock and Watch Makers and their Work* (1894), but comparison of the different authorities shows discrepancies in dates—see Baillie's listing of the Pinchbeck family.

After the complex problems set by the bullion value of the gold case those of the more common silver case are fairly straightforward, providing, of course, that the marks have not been obscured by wear or over-energetic buffing. The lion passant and the hallmark, together with the casemaker's initials, are usually to be found both inside the dome and inside the back. The mark on the stem and the bow may be different both in maker and date, suggesting that these parts were made separately and in bulk elsewhere. Not every part of the case is marked so meticulously as is invariable with gold. Clutton and Daniels significantly remark that "Silver cases were seldom hallmarked before 1740". This point has already been made in regard to early eighteenth-century watches, and we are left with an unfortunate gap in the exact dating of the early watch. The sovereign's head, altered in direction in alternate reigns, rarely appears in my watches. It only came into use in 1784 and indicated that duty had been paid on a silver article. Watch cases were exempted in 1798.

There are two standards of purity for silver. Sterling ·925 is that most commonly used, but this is never stamped on the silver case. Between the years 1697 and 1720 the standard of silver was raised to ·9584 in order to combat the practice of using silver coin of the realm as raw material for conversion into articles of plate. Silver of this standard, known as "Britannia Standard" is marked with the figure of Britannia and the lion's head erased. It is rarely if ever seen on watch cases. The few Swiss cases in my possession are stamped ·935 silver.

Though English silver has been carefully stamped from earliest times, a much less stringent standard has been applied to silver watch cases.

While the names of some of the more popular casemakers are known and appear in Baillie, there is, unfortunately (as far as I know) nothing like the complete list to which the collector can refer, as with the makers of gold and silver plate. The short list of monograms given by Baillie refers mainly to German clockmakers, and to try to pick a casemaker from Baillie's general lists with only initials as a clue is usually unrewarding.

The initials A.L.D. figure prominently in the third common casemaking material—namely, rolled gold. Dennison's final business success probably depended on the development of this process in America about 1880 and its spread within a few years to this country. The books report very little about rolled or filled gold cases but my collection shows it to have been predominantly a feature of the Edwardian and neo-Georgian social scene. Technically it is a matter of fusing a very thin plate of gold on each side of a much heavier plate of brass or composition. From this the case shapes are cut, worked and polished without apparently much difficulty. The work is, therefore, indistinguishable from gold because on the surface it really is gold. The only way a rolled gold case can be "spotted" on superficial examination by the collector is by seeing patches where the gold has been worn away. This particularly happens on the underside of the bow where the attached chain rubbed. Of course, there is no hallmark, but there is a legal requirement both in America and this country that such cases carry a clearly worded trade description stamped on the inside face of the dome. The wording is usually on the lines of: "Guaranteed to be made of two plates of gold with a layer of composition between and warranted to wear for X years". In some, only the number of years of warranted wear is given. Swiss cases may state simply and honestly "rolled gold" and guarantee a certain number of years' wear.

The misleading part of the trade description hinges on the use of the word "gold". It is specified as being plates of "solid gold" or of 10 or 14-carat gold. Many a widow has been sadly disillusioned when she came to sell her husband's gold watch to find it worth very little. The small amount of gold can be reclaimed but the cost of doing so is high and hardly economic. The current price of a scrapped gold-filled case is less than that of a silver case, though with today's bullion prices this may rise. However, looked at from the practical angle, there are at least three points which count heavily in favour of the otherwise dubious rolled gold case.

While one would expect a high-class movement to be accorded the dignity of a gold case, this has never been an invariable rule even from early days. An eighteenth-century verge movement from a good stable can be found in a silver or pinchbeck case, but the collector of today is more likely to find the cheaper cased watches. It depended as usual on the depth of the customer's pocket and what he could afford when he gave his order to the retailing watchmaker for onward passage to the casemaker. The same factors continued through the last century with the hand-made watches and cases, and they certainly operated in full when machine-made watches and cases arrived. The retailer could supply a movement of high or low class in silver, rolled gold or gold with, of course, wide differences in price. The collector who must be primarily interested in the movement will, of course, not allow himself to be overinfluenced by the wrapping. He is as likely to find the high-class modern movement in a rolled gold case as in gold, though he may recase it later as befits its status.

The second point is that the warranty of so many years daily use without obvious wear is a good one. The A.L.D. case is in three grades. The Star carries a ten-year guarantee with a star symbol. The Moon has a twenty-year guarantee marked with a crescent moon and star (and often the sun symbol). The Sun case is guaranteed for twenty-five years and carries the sun, moon and star mark. A twenty-year warranty is virtually a lifetime's wear and the twenty-five-year can become an heirloom without giving away the secret—only the ten-year cases are liable to show wear. Some of the Swiss cases only give a five-year guarantee but would still seem to have been exported to this country. From America come cases made by the Illinois company, Wadsworth's and Keystone, but there is little or no evidence in my watches of any other British manufacturer than the Dennison Watch Case Company.

Each Dennison case has a stamped number and it is believed that the last two figures indicate the year of manufacture, though this may not be the year in which they were used. This can be very helpful for dating purposes, since there is no hallmark. As far as I can check from the serial numbers of Waltham movements, this supposition about the last two figures may well be correct. It is a rather crude method because we do not know how long the movement or the case may have been in stockrooms before they were married. For instance, one of my watches, a fifteen-jewel Waltham with a micrometer adjustment, shows a movement number of nineteen-million-odd. The case number is 535413 suggesting April 1913, and the nineteenth million begins to be found in 1915 in this country. A Waltham seven-jewel movement is numbered in the twenty-third million and the ten-year case shows a number ending in which 25 appears below the main number line. The twenty-third million appeared in 1925. Another Waltham seven-jewel movement number is also in the twenty-third million and again 25 appears below the main case number line. It would need many Dennison cases to prove the point and it would seem that the system only came into the case numbers about, say, 1905. It does not apply to other manufacturers as far as I know.

The third point about rolled gold cases is a rather mixed one, in that a rolled gold case will comfortably pass as gold until one reads the disclaimer or fails to find the hallmark. The deception worries me as it must have worried people who had to make social estimates in the Victorian days of class rigidity. Whatever a gentleman is or was, an essential part of the definition was a gold watch. It must have been very disturbing to pillars of society to find that the juniors also appeared to have gold watches. It would be impossible for either to inform his friends that his was real, or the other that his was not. Perhaps this was one of the telling blows struck at the hierarchy of class.

In this country the final twentieth-century case was completely plain with rarely some engine-turned pattern on the back. Some of my American cases show that chased decoration persisted longer in rolled gold cases, with some designs in different coloured alloys in gold cases. It is interesting that the single silver cases of the nineteenth century in my collection almost invariably featured on the back of the case a blank shield or badge for engraving the owner's initials. If such badges were for this purpose, none of my watches now show initials. However, since the shield and its inevitable surrounding garter are raised in the design they may all have worn and rubbed away over the many years of pocket living. Perhaps this motif of shield and garter was universally adopted by the casemakers to show the world that here was an example of the renowned English lever. The fashion fell away at the end of the nineteenth century and appears very much less often on the chronographs. As far as the last hundred years of the verge was concerned (1750 to 1850) the plain case was the rule of manufacture.

Slightly different was the Victorian and Edwardian habit of inscribing one's monogram in expert engraving over the whole back of the case. Less common, for obvious reasons, was the habit of engraving one's family crest and motto. It is difficult to say at this distance whether the monogrammed watch was an egotistical gesture or primarily an anti-theft safeguard. Certainly for the first owner it was good evidence of ownership, but as far as we are concerned today this worthy person is long dead and unidentifiable, and the monogram poses the collector with a problem. It should not do so on logical grounds because all today's pocket watches are manifestly not only secondhand, they may have had many previous owners. However, human nature is not logical. The individual buyer does not want somebody else's monogram on his watch and the dealer will offer less for one when buying. The collector must be aware of this lower market value, and if he is then he will get something with added interest at a lower price.

In my view the monogram is an integral part of the case decoration and period and should be left *in situ*. However, the cunning of their design and engraving is that they are very superficial and shallow and can fairly easily be buffed off by a competent engraver. Some of the gold of the case is lost, of course, but the back still has a satisfactory thickness upon which the new owner can put his own monogram—assuming, of course, that the case is not one of those paper-thin affairs of Continental origin—usually of 14K standard. A.L.D. also put some thinnish cases out in the economy days of the 1920s and 1930s, these are marked Special. However, the engravers were clever enough of hand to put monograms with equal frequency upon rolled gold cases without apparently breaching the thin gold plate. Whether these could be buffed off is a matter of doubt, perhaps it could in a twenty or twenty-five year case but one would expect the area to wear through far in advance of the rest of the case. I have one rolled gold case in which initials have been deeply cut and, as one might expect, brown corrosion has spread outwards from the letters between the gold plate and the inner composition plate.

16

The Recased Watch

SOONER or later the active and enterprising collector is bound to meet this problem and, as some of my descriptions of individual watches show, it has faced me on several occasions. It is worth going into the question in a little detail since there is little or nothing published about this. The expert will simply say "the case is not original" and leave it at that. Ethically, recasing is condemned because the piece might be passed off to a buyer as intact, in its original state and wholly authentic. Its value and true price would be very much impaired if subsequently it was shown that the case belonged originally to some other watch. This is also true of long-case clocks where the case wears out long before the movement, but here substitution may be very difficult to prove. In watches the need for recasing arises in both directions. On the one hand, the verge movement may wear out before the case: or, what is more likely, it may be irreparable because of high cost and the lack of a craftsman able to remake some part. On the other hand, a gold case may have been scrapped because of its bullion value, leaving behind a movement in good repair and possibly by a prestige maker. We may then have the position where the good movement could well be substituted for the worn-out one if the two matched reasonably well. The temptation to do this is particularly strong with movements of well-known makers and it is here that the collector must look into the provenance of the case just as carefully as that of the movement. In fact, if he proposes to spend any large sum on buying an antique watch it is advisable for him to take it home on approval for full study first and to get a good guarantee covering any subsequent doubts about its full authenticity. It is easy to say this but, on looking back, most of my watches have been bought much more casually, gambling on the skill of my watchmaker to get me out of all but the most serious blunders.

With the high price of bullion today there is again a great deal of gold case scrapping. Luckily this is confined to the more modern watches, the value of the good older watch being fully known. The collector can come by interesting movements as a result. The greatest destruction, however, was seen in the early 1930s when this country went off the gold standard in the depression years. This massacre of the watches in the "gold rush" remains a horrible fact of history. There was relatively little interest in horology at that time, but there can be little doubt that thousands of classical watches which we would revere today were destroyed then. The older dealers tell me that under the counters of jewellers' shops there were biscuit tins full of these movements, from which there came a constant ticking. The going price at that time was about sixpence each and at that they were sold to the repairing trade for cannibalization. My friend Mr. Stanley Smith, when an apprentice, used to spend his meagre lunch money to rescue some outstanding piece from the biscuit tins. Today the few survivors command much more realistic prices. Probably the rape of the 1930s came too late for new silver cases to be made and too early for many people to realize what a horological heritage was being thrown away. The late Professor D. S. Torrens, the noted horologist of Trinity College, Dublin, was one of the few who attempted to salvage some of these pieces.

Bearing in mind that all the older cases were hand-made to fit movements of many different shapes and sizes, the chances of finding a marriageable pair is really quite slim. In verges, however, opportunities do arise and this is the field in which one should be on the look-out for substitution. The first point to check is the hallmark and the casemaker's monogram which must be the same on both inner and outer case. Outer cases do get lost and this has happened in two of my watches. More important is to see that the case hallmark corresponds to the movement-maker's period and known dates. It should be remembered that the dates given in Baillie do not necessarily cover the whole of the maker's active life and often do not include date of birth or death. This may leave wide margins. Another explanation is that a movement might lie in stock (already engraved) for an indefinite time before it was sold and sent to be cased. The reverse, however, cannot be allowed, i.e., the case date cannot anticipate the date by which it can be calculated that the apprentice is at least out of his time. A tactful re-encasement would therefore use a case within the movement maker's period, though it must be remembered that the last date in Baillie's list is not always indicative of the cessation of business, or indeed death, unless this is stated. The assay office is also to be noted. A provincial casemaker may well send his work to London to be stamped but it looks a little odd for a London finished movement to have a case stamped in a provincial office. If we had a dictionary of casemakers' initials we would have another line of enquiry to help in establishing whether the case was original or not.

The next thing to examine is the fit of the movement in the case. A fair degree of wear on the top hinge is to be expected, but the movement should fit fairly exactly when in place. There may be evidence that the hinge on either side has been altered—the movement part of the hinge is merely pinned on and can be exchanged for one that marries into the pattern on the case. It is not easy to coax an oversize movement into a smaller case and there may be signs that easing has been carried out. More usually, the movement will be seen to be too small and instead of fitting the front plate rebate it is sloppy. It may be seen, too, that a new cut has had to be made in the case rim to take the spring catch which is in a different position. All these alterations are, of course, well within the capacity of the case repairer. What is much more difficult is to match the winding hole in the dome of the new inner case with the winding arbor. Often this calls for a completely new winding hole and the old hole has to be filled in, a repair that is difficult to conceal completely. In other cases it will be seen that the original round winding hole has had to be extended to an oval shape to allow the key to fit.

As an example of recasing one might take the Mudge cylinder watch that was offered to me at a reasonable enough price, the seller knowing that the case was not original. The movement was characteristically of Mudge design with correct numerals, beetle and poker hands, centre seconds hand and stop-work. The movement number (6240) placed its date between 1759 and 1765. The gilding and jewelling was good. The inner case fitted well but was hallmarked 1823 and a very amateurish attempt had been made to alter this to 1723 and to amend the characteristics of the leopard's head. The outer case was shagreen-covered on pinchbeck but the stem groove was too large for the present inner case. My reason for not buying was a broken cylinder, which would be very difficult to have remade, rather than the obvious recasing. (I have a prejudice against collecting pieces which cannot be put into working order.) Had the movement been viable then the ethics of recasing appear in another light, providing, of course, that there is no attempt to pass the piece off as original.

From the horological point of view much of our information comes from classical examples which exist only in the form of movements (sometimes mutilated) which for one reason or another have lost their cases. My own material includes a large number of movements ranging from ancient to quite modern. Even if they have been overhauled, are working, and perhaps quite intact, they languish in their boxes and make very little impact. Certainly they are far less impressive than those that can be handled and worn because they are cased. Though a movement has value and a price (no doubt they will be much sought after in later years) it is far less than that of the complete watch. Though it remains unethical to put a movement in another case with a view to misleading a future purchaser, on practical grounds this gives the discarded movement a new lease of life and usefulness. However, as been pointed out, though this may have been reasonably feasible previously when both cases and movements were more numerous it is unlikely that such opportunities will present now.

One final point might be made in regard to the modern machine-made cases in which, within certain limitations, there is interchangeability. Here case-swopping can hardly be unethical as the case speaks for itself as to date, period and material. The limitations are firstly that a hunter movement will not, of course, suit an open-face case and vice versa. In the hunter the stem enters at a three o'clock position to allow the thumb to press the winding button. The open face is read with the winding button uppermost in the twelve o'clock position. The other problem is the length of the stem, which seems to vary between certain American and Swiss movements. So it may be found that though the movement fits the case the hands cannot be set. A watchmaker may be able to overcome this.

However skilful a watch repairer may be he cannot be expected to be able to make a new case spring, a new hinge, or a new catch to a verge case. There are even fewer men who can now make the complete case and recase a movement. A friend of mine did have a silver case made for a tourbillon movement at a cost of several hundred pounds. To have a new gold case made today the client would have to produce his own bullion to keep the cost within bounds, but even so the time and labour needed for fashioning will be major items. It might be thought worthwhile to rehouse some of the more modern and stereotyped gold cased movements in silver or rolled gold cases to provide the bullion.

17

The Dress Watch and the Goliath

THESE two early twentieth-century types rate barely a mention in any of the text-books though the Goliath is noted and illustrated by de Carle in his *Encyclopedia*. They are simply bygones but quite likely enough to turn up to puzzle the collector, and therefore they merit description (illustration No. 135). It is doubtful if dress watches were ever made by the English trade. They appeared on the scene at a time when few English watches were being made and most if not all were imported from Switzerland or America.

Most dress watches have the traditional machine-made case, but this is too bulky. Usually the dome is omitted and the case is slimmed by designing out the middle of the body. A slim movement presented no design problems. The winding button and bow were small and streamlined. The case was fancy or decorated, and the hands and dial may be elaborate. Worn with a slim gold or plated chain it was an elegant piece of masculine jewellery for evening wear. One would expect the case to be invariably in gold, but rolled gold cases are quite common, no doubt on the double basis of being exposed to little wear and the extra expense of buying two gold watches. Silver would certainly never be used.

These pieces have always attracted me because of their good taste and the fact that they usually have high-class movements. They turn up much less commonly than the full-sized pocket watch, and there are sixteen examples in the collection. Their use was probably limited to the Edwardian period, but they cannot be accurately dated because there are no hallmarks as there are no English pieces and none was cased in this country. The American firms of Waltham and Elgin made eight of the sixteen pieces. Waltham used high-class movements with 15, 17 and 19 jewels, of which two were in rolled gold cases of American make. One was in a 14K American case, but the other provides our only hallmark, being cased by A.L.D. in Birmingham in 1926. The four Elgin movements were only 7-jewel movements in rolled gold cases, though the standard of decoration was good. The Swiss movements were all fully jewelled—

Omega, Recta, Persee and Zenith being the main names. Only one was in a gold case (14K) but the design and finish were always first-class.

On the whole it was the Swiss who dominated the scene and wearing a dress watch was an imported Continental habit. If the Victorian Englishman wore a different watch in the evening it would probably be simply a smaller-sized pocket watch. The aim of the dress watch was, however, something different. It was to be so slim and elegant that it could be worn in a black or white waistcoat without spoiling the lines of a well-cut evening suit. Possibly expensive tailors insisted that their clients wore it.

At the beginning of this century society was sharply divided between those who dressed regularly for dinner each night (even in the jungle) and those who had not crossed this social barrier. The novels of the day were quite specific that Victorian prosperity was not acceptable socially until this change was made. World War I very much curtailed the evening dressing habit and World War II virtually swept it away. Now we only dress for an evening function and wear a wrist watch.

The lady's watch, which is merely a scaled-down pocket watch, is quite different. This was worn on a brooch or carried on a neck chain, and few were made in England. The example quite commonly met with is a cheap French or Swiss cylinder while Walthams had made the size 10 movement for many years. These should be carefully avoided by the collector. Not only are they always out of repair, but they are rarely reparable, and cause endless trouble. The exact size of a movement is measured across the plates and it has to be remembered that the case adds considerably to the over-all outside measurement. In modern movements the deck watch and the chronograph range between size 24 and 20. The ordinary pocket watch is either size 18 or 16, and the lady's watch size 10. The dress watch is usually size 12.

The goliath watch or watch-clock (illustrations Nos. 135–137) was designed as a bedside clock and also has an interesting place in social history; the collector should always be interested in picking up these rather rare pieces. The outer cases are usually square, leather covered and silver faced. Inside they are lined with velvet and have the usual raised ring to hold the watch with a cut-out at twelve o'clock to accommodate the larger bow. Illustration No. 126 is of a very neat small silver case designed to take a gentleman's pocket watch and have it stand on the bedside table.

The watches themselves were massive, far too heavy to be carried in any pocket. My examples vary from $2\frac{1}{2}$ to 3 inches across the case but (possibly as some obscure Swiss music hall joke) they were reported as sometimes attaining diameters of 6 to 9 inches or even larger. Since all my watches are Swiss made they were imported and had the outer travelling case added in this country.

Only one of the watches has a silver case, presumably because a very large amount of silver would be needed. This is a fine piece with an over-all diameter of 2¾ inches and a foreign case stamped ·935 Silver, and carrying two appropriate stylized bears. In total it weighs just under 10 ounces (troy) while another, not in silver, also takes the spring balance down to its 10-ounce stop. It should be remembered that foreign cases have no hallmark indicating the year of submission to assay. The movement is a well-finished high-class 15-jewel with, exceptionally, an eight-day run (marked on the dial). Otherwise it has the characteristic heavy bow and large winding button and the side hand-set with olivettes. More usually the movements were thirty-hour, and were wound and set each night. They are all of robust well-made 15-jewel standard in good condition, and after overhaul keep very good time. There does not appear to be any standard layout for the movement and it is interesting that the escape wheels are not all clubtoothed but of the English rachet or spur type. Possibly the Swiss did not adopt the clubtooth until later in this century.

The goliaths often present merely as a watch, since the travelling case may have worn out and been lost. Under these conditions, such as a large heavy watch without any chain, wear on the bow is difficult to explain. The collector will wonder about the exact purpose served in the design of such a large watch and may toy with the idea of a deck watch. However, all these pieces are Swiss identified by the thick black numerals and the side hand-setting. When intact the cases have a silver embellished front and from the hallmark, mostly Birmingham, this dates the pieces in the Edwardian period. They were the requirements of the perpetual traveller or the perpetual guest such as my widowed or maiden aunts who, not being able to maintain a home of their own, divided their time between the homes of their relatives or genteel boarding houses.

18
Pocket Watch Accessories

IT is hardly surprising that around the central figure of the watch itself have grown up a number of adjuncts and hangers-on. Most of these have at least some use or ornament and a few notes will be valuable to the collector; particularly since little attention is given to them in the standard texts unless they are of a decorative rating. As watches became more reliable and essentially workaday instruments they became plain and functional. They ceased to be carried on chains round the neck or waist as jewellery and disappeared into the pocket, and their status rested on the accuracy of the movement. While it is true that there are collectors who confine themselves to individual accessories such as keys or watch-papers, this can be of little interest to the watch collector. Those who collect watch-cocks for their intricate workmanship must not be surprised if they are regarded with horror by those who revere the whole watch. Even the watch-paper and the key would be better employed in their proper places.

Speaking of keys first: none of the elaborate chased, jewelled, cranked, or tipsy cranked keys figure in my collection. They did not present in my collecting experience and had they done so they would have been very expensive. They are to be found in association with the high-grade antique watches, but it is rare in older watches for the original key to be linked with an old watch. Daily use use leads to a great deal of wear and the splitting of the shank, and it is possible to fit a new business end by driving out the pin, but most owners would simply buy a new standard key. Keys are still made and sold today in one sterotyped pattern. No one size ever became standard and twelve different fittings are still made, the number being stamped on. It is impossible to say at what date this range of twelve sizes became adopted and it might well be assumed that the older watchmakers pleased themselves in regard to the size of the winding square they used. Whether there was a separate trade of keymaking is another mystery. From an early stage in my collecting I found it useful to build up a stock of watch keys of the older types and designs by pestering dealers and hunting in flea markets. It seems incongruous to team up an old watch with a key made yesterday. Representative designs of commonplace keys can be seen in illustration No. 120. There is a short note on watch keys in Britten's *Old Clocks and Watches* (1932 edition), but there is little additional information elsewhere. One would have expected a key to incorporate a swivel so that one could wind smoothly without tangling up the chain, but not all have this advantage.

Universal keys were of great help to the watch repairer and the simplest was the one with either five or six legs. In all my examples one or more of the legs are missing and, furthermore, none are numbered; it would seem that the odd numbers of the range of twelve are eliminated. In any case the experienced tradesman can usually pick the size he needs by merely looking at the square. (It might be noted here that when watches became cheaper and more numerous even winding keyless watches could be a terrible chore for a watchmaker who had to rate dozens of them before retailing. Fingers would become so sore that special winding machines were invented for this purpose.) More usually the watchmaker used the Birch key—three variations of which are shown in illustration No. 121—the central example with a black wooden handle being the usual type. This is spring-loaded with jaws which grip any size square. Birch was an American and his keys may still be bought. Each one carries the inscription "John S. Birch, U.S. Patent, April 13th. 69. May 23d. 76", giving the exact provenance of this benefactor of the watchmaker's bench. The other two examples are more primitive and not so easy to work with. One is marked "Pat. Aprl. 13. 69" and the other "Birch's Patent, Licensed by B.P.O." A fourth example, much patched up, has a stamp "Birch's patent U.S. May 23d. 76". A Birch key is a useful companion when looking for watches. In *It's About Time* Chamberlain tells us that watch keys were a constant embarassment to their users because invariably they became full of dust and lint to such an extent this sometimes had to be removed with a pin before the watch could be wound. A dustless key was marketed in America, having a rectangular opening through it to prevent blockage, but this seems never to have reached this country and is not represented in my collection. In 1867 the dustproof watchkey factory was bought by K. and D., a watch tool company. The K. stood for Frank B. Kendrick (the active partner) and the D. for a dentist named Davies (the sleeping partner). In 1894 K. and D. bought the Birch key and subsequently manufactured it until well into the twentieth century.

From keys to watch chains via the watch fob. In the form generally handed down (see illustration No. 122) this is of black *moiré* silk, sporting the owner's seal at one end. They may, of course, be much more ornate and dressy. The watch rested in a fob pocket in the waistband of the trousers which were worn with a short double-breasted waistcoat. This was thought to be more thief-proof than the waistcoat pocket and one can visualize the well-covered owner having to breathe in before he could draw the watch from the waistband. Fashions became drab when Victoria came to the throne—the waistcoats became longer and the fob was no longer accessible.

Next the watch chain became the mode, usually double, and linked always with the name of Albert, the Prince Consort (see illustrations Nos. 123–130). He may have brought in the style in 1840 specifically from Saxe-Coburg or more vaguely from the Continental scene. Certainly it lived to the end of the pocket-watch era. The chains were made of various metals from the workman's steel chain through the silver and gold plate to the gold. Dress watches were tethered with delicate traceries in gold or white gold. There was great variation in design and particularly in weight, and an enormous air of respectability was imparted by a heavy double gold albert across a capacious aldermanic belly. The most popular would seem to have been the simple horse-curb link, but the link-and-fetter suited a taller, slimmer man. In fact the watch chain was one of the few ways in which the conventional male could project his personal image.

I have by no means attempted to collect a chain to suit each particular type of watch in the collection but rather a selection of the types in common use. Most of these can be seen in illustration Nos. 115–122, and a word might be given to each.

1. The modern chain made for today's pocket watch is a single slim affair ending in a round button to fit in the left lapel buttonhole. The metal is probably not silver; more probably it is gilt.
2. After the First World War a simple leather leash with a buttonhole bar was favoured, the fittings being silver, gilt or gold. Sometimes this was plaited and occasionally it had a buckle for the buttonhole.
3. A common Victorian "chain" was made of black woven horsehair with metal ends; this may have been for mourning.
4. The working man's watch might only have a steel, copper or gunmetal chain.
5. Gilt chains were often to be found, usually in fancy designs rather than a solid link, as the wear in these would soon cut through the thin layer of gold.
6. Dress watches were worn with thin fancy chains which though unostentatious were of red or white gold.
7. The majority of my collection are of silver bought at a time when they sold merely by weight as scrap silver. Stamped in every link, they varied from the inconspicuous to heavy pieces which might scale up to 4 ounces.

The simple horse-curb link was mostly used, link-and-fetter and fancy designs being less favoured. The links always show very definite wear. Where the albert was double the free end might carry the key, a vesta matchbox or a sovereign-case. From the centre bar there was usually a short chain designed for a medallion, a small compass, a Masonic emblem or a charm. The medallion most properly used was a prize for some sport and in illustration No. 128 can be seen some of these tokens of sporting prowess. Most of the hallmarks are Edwardian or late Victorian and always from the Birmingham Mint. It was no doubt considered most unsporting to wear a gilt-silver chain even with a rolled gold watch—the gold chain had to be the real thing. Having made some experiments in gilding these silver chains, it is difficult to avoid a brassy appearance—a sure mark of the cad or bounder.

8. Gold watch chains are, at today's bullion price, very expensive and have always carried a premium above their actual weight, by which they are always valued. An 18-carat English lever watch with matching chain and trinket will be priced at several hundred pounds in accordance with its intrinsic value. For such a sum a collector could still find much of interest in the antique watch market. An additional premium is that such chains are in great demand for ladies' bracelets and charm bracelets. For obvious reasons they are rarely so massive as those made in silver. The design is usually the simple curb or the link-and-fetter; exuberance in pattern was not in good taste. The embellishment was quieter—a seal or a mounted guinea or two-pound piece. No gentleman could be allowed to be a fop; the only jewellery permitted was the watch chain, the cuff links and perhaps (rather dashing) a tiepin.

The demise of the pocket watch followed that of the waistcoat for without a waistcoat pocket it is very difficult to carry a pocket watch safely. If a watch is carried in the open-topped breast pocket with a chain to the lapel buttonhole it will sooner or later fall out, with unfortunate results. It is reasonably safe in a uniform jacket with two flapped and buttoned breast pockets. The chain can unobtrusively cross the inch or two between the pockets, but will be an awkward obstacle when taking the jacket off. The only suitable alternative to the wrist watch today would be a return to the fob pocket in the waistband of the trousers. Any pocket is, of course, a dust trap and the careful pocket-watch man would always cosset his watch in a chamois leather cover. These are still sold today, though it is not easy to find one large enough for the bigger watches. They can be easily washed and the fluff and dust removed. A superior version of very good chamois leather is also sold, circular rather than U-shaped, and possibly intended for the dress watch. It will be recalled that fingerprints should not be left on the dome when closing a watch and the chamois leather is useful for removing them.

Since we spend a third of our life in bed the question arises as to what to do with a pocket watch at bedtime. (Most owners were in the fixed habit of winding their watches before going to bed but it has long been suggested that there would be better timekeeping if the winding was done in the morning.) No doubt some put the watch in a drawer but the majority left it on the dressing table where it was reasonably safe from accident, though cold. Others hung it above their heads on the brass bedstead. Under the pillow it was warm but evasive. Proper watch stands seem to have been rarely used but they can be found in all forms and shapes. An old version is a box with bevelled glass sides where the watch rests on a velvet or satin cushion. The collector should always be on the look-out for them.

19

The Provenance of a Watch

WHEN we add a new watch to our collection we should naturally want to know as much as possible about its type, its escapement, its maker, its period, its age and its approximate date of manufacture. In many instances all this can be ascertained fairly easily, provided one learns to use the various sources of information. There are many pieces of evidence that can be assembled, but naturally it is vital that they all agree. If one clue has to be abandoned to make the verdict unanimous one must try to work out an explanation as to why this fact is misleading. In the main there are three approaches. The first is the general design and type of escapement used in the piece. The second is the hallmark on the case, assuming it is hallmarked. Thirdly, there is reference to lists of recorded makers, so long as the movement is signed.

The experienced horologist can, of course, make a shrewd guess at the age of a watch simply by looking at it, but he is relying on experience that the beginner has still to acquire. This book has covered in detail the various periods of development over the last two hundred or so years. The periods of time during which certain types of watch were being made were not, however, sharp cut. There was inevitably a slow change of fashion and reluctance to give up old ideas, and we do not know how individual makers reacted. One may have been a go-ahead innovator, while another might have found it impossible to learn new techniques and continued to make a movement that had always satisfied his father's customers. While London was sensitive to Continental progress and Lancashire sometimes had good ideas of its own, it took time before the country watchmakers (and clockmakers) were willing to follow the lead. As an example, Mudge made the first lever escapement in 1769 but few took any interest in it before 1800. Then there was another lull in interest until about 1830 when the Lancashire men took it up with massive support. So, too, the verge continued to be made for many years after this and my youngest verge has a case date of 1868. Though the going barrel was in use in America from about 1850 the fusee was almost exclusive in this country until about 1880 and I have examples made even after 1900. So at any given date one can find several different types of watches in production even though the general consensus was for the more modern type. Allowing, however, for this spread, the outside appearance should fix the period even though the hallmark may be a bit of a surprise when it comes to be read.

Accurate recognition of the type of escapement is a matter of experience but very roughly speaking, as far as English watches are concerned, if the movement is not a verge then it is a lever. The rarer escapements, which are dealt with in a separate chapter, are more difficult for the beginner to work out as I know from my own experience and from seeing others' mistakes. It is by no means easy, even with a watchmaker's glass, to be quite sure what is going on in the confined space between the plates. The main thing is to be able to see that it is not a verge and not a lever and keep at the back of one's mind that the movement may have been altered, e.g., leverized. Judging from my own experience, the likelihood that the collector will stumble on an unusual escapement is remote. The most likely is the cylinder or the duplex, recognizable from the side view of the respective escape wheels. The clubfoot verge has the chaff-cutter action. The rack action of the rack lever is also fairly easily seen and the lunate counterbalance at the outer end of the lever is obvious. These levers almost invariably had the word "patent" engraved on the balance cock (they were made under Litherland's patent) but this legend can also be found on movements boasting only a simple lever mechanism.

However, leaving the unusual movement on one side and recognizing that there was considerable lag in taking up new ideas we can be more certain of the earliest date of some changes It might be helpful to try to summarize the changes over the centuries so long as it is kept in mind that no date is hard-and-fast. The following list is set out on the basis of recognition of the period of a watch by superficial examination of case-style and movement.

1900 onwards. Plain machine-made case, open-faced or hunter style, button wind, sleeve hand-setting, and very rarely of English manufacture. Movement divided-three-quarter top plate, club-toothed escape wheel and simple or complicated regulating index.

1890 About this year the keyless button wind appeared for the first time in association with the side setting of the hands. Nearly all were of English manufacture with the side action lever and spur-toothed escape wheels. The top plate was full, three-quarters, or sometimes half-plate. The fusee had become a rarity and the dummy barrel was common. The chronograph watch was now becoming the fashion and the over-all tendency was towards the clumsy, ungainly watch.

1880 The appearance in English-made watches of the going barrel and the eclipse of the fusee and chain. Heavy cases reappeared. Key wind invariable in this country. The dome in this case fixed, with holes for winding and hand-setting. The movement still swung forward from the top hinge and dust covers were universal. The back opened by means of a push-piece on top of the stem for winding and setting.

Mid-century. Lever watches were slim, single cased and well designed, with sometimes a decorated dial. They were key wound and the hand-setting was on a shallow square on the centre arbor. The chronometer escapement was being produced but it was rare and expensive, while cylinders were out of fashion. The verge was still a popular country watch and mostly double cased and bulky. The movement was mass-produced, often with a painted dial and unsigned. All types of movement swung forward and all, apart from the verge, had dust covers.

1830–1840 The advent of the simple lever escapement and the run-down of the verge. From the outset the levers were slim and used only a single case, allowing the increased use of the hunting case. The seconds hand and dial also became more common. The regulating index began to migrate to the top of the cock, which became plain, while engraving on the top plate was less frequent.

1800–1830 While the verge remained predominant, this was the heyday of the unorthodox inventive escapement in which the rack lever proved the cheapest and most reliable, while the more expensive cylinder was thought to be the watch of the future. Verges were bulky and usually double case though the single consular case was introduced.

1800 For some reason this proved quite a turning point in verge design in several respects. The case became heavier and larger to the nineteenth-century pattern. The bows became deeper or simply rounded rather than D-shaped. The hinge of the outer case was faired into the circumference. Tompion's rosette regulator was replaced by the index arm and quadrant. The setting-up square for the spring barrel was phased out, the decorated cock and top plate became more restrained.

The Eighteenth Century. For most of this period the design of the verge was fairly stable—small, neat, and easily recognizable. It entered the century fat and rounded with a champlevé dial, and a sprung balance, and though it was no doubt uncomfortable there, it was carried in the pocket.

Having done as much as we can to date the watch by means of the approximate period and type of escapement the next evidence comes from the hallmark stamped on the case. This can, and should be, a very simple matter and it might be thought that there was very little to be said about it. Experience shows, however, that sooner or later discrepancies arise, and that there is more to the simple process of identification than meets the eye. It must first be explained that the date on the case is not complete proof that the movement was made within a year or two of that date. When speaking of the age of any watch it is best to say "case-dated 1782" rather than "made in 1782". As has been pointed out, it is not easy to be sure that this is the real and original case and sometimes, of course, the hallmark may not be the same on inner and outer case. You may find a case with two different hallmarks side by side. The hallmark, though it seems so simple and foolproof, should be accepted with reserve. In the case of gold and silver plate antiques, excellent forgeries have been found, though this is less likely in watches. Another point is that since only gold and silver are so marked, watch cases in gilt or pinchbeck carry only the casemaker's initial.

In reading the hallmark it is usually sufficient to rely on *Bradbury's Book of Hallmarks*. This also gives guidance on gold marks and carats—but it is important to read the accompanying notes and historical facts. Lists of hallmarks are to be found in the various editions of Britten, but the most comprehensive book is *English Goldsmiths and their Marks* by Sir Charles J. Jackson (1905). There also *Old English Plate* by W. J. Cripps (1978) and Chaffers' *Handbook to Hallmarks on Gold and Silver Plate* (1924) which can be of further help.

The simplest and commonest mistake to make when using these lists is to refer the letter to the wrong mint. Many of the assay offices have now closed. Significantly in my collection there are no assay marks other than London, Chester and Birmingham (in that order of frequency), which strongly suggests that there was little or no manufacture in Scotland or Ireland, nor probably in Wales either. The Lancashire trade went to Chester.

Another practical problem for a collector arises when the date letter is worn. This is usually due not to fair wear and tear but to an unusually energetic "buffing-up" by a case or watch repairer who wants to remove scratches and repairer's marks. Another difficulty is that the shield does not always stay constant in shape through the many years that the alphabetical sequence has to run; no doubt because the punch wears out and is carelessly recut. The sequences do not run standard lengths in each mint. London favours stopping at U, Birmingham likes to carry on to Z, and Chester is quite irregular. Though efforts are made by each assay office to keep the letter style different in each sequence they were not always successful. London has a bad example of this. The sequence starting in 1776 is almost identical with that starting forty years later in 1816. On silver plate this does not matter as the duty mark (the Monarch's head) helps identification, but duty on watches was abolished in 1798. The shield is the same and many of the letters are distinguishable only by minor changes in the serif, easily removed by wear. Some letters are identical.

It was at one time usual for imported cases to be re-assayed in this country after import but this seems to have gone by the board some years ago. The re-assay mark and the marks of foreign origin are listed in the hallmark handbook. In the main, however, we seem for the last hundred years to have accepted foreign assay marks such as 14K from America and Switzerland as well as the standard of silver purity. However, it must be realized that there is not (to my knowledge) any system of hallmarking outside this country that conveys the date at which the case was submitted to assay.

After getting what help we can from the markings of the case we then turn to lists of makers. It has to be noted that the initials of the casemaker cannot help in dating because we have no lists of them. Britten notes that by an Act of 1777 the name and place of abode of the maker were required to be inscribed on watches made in this country. This was, of course, usually done from the very first examples (and, less frequently, on clocks). This may have been ordered, with penalties for forgeries when detected, to discourage lesser makers from engraving and attributing their work to that of prestige makers. This was quite prevalent in this country and in France at the time. It is also said that forgeries were imported from other parts of the Continent. Naturally this can cause a great deal of trouble when such watches turn up today. By the nineteenth century the law was either repealed or ignored and anonymous mass-produced watches became common. It also raises the question of who actually made the watch: eventually the name on the top plate or the dial was simply that of the retailer. This has been a vexed matter from very early on in the history of the watch, and many quite reputable names are merely those of the finisher, dependent on prior work of many other people. Baillie attempts, as a result of wide research, to draw the line.

There are three sources of makers' names. Britten came first in 1894. Then Baillie enlarged on Britten in 1929. Thirdly, today's researchers are compiling lists, usually on a county basis. Most of these books are concerned with clockmakers only and are of no help. In *Clock and Watch Makers in Wales*, by Iorworth C. Peats, it is almost impossible to sort out the actual watchmakers from the repairers and the clockmakers. There is, however, a list of watches by Welsh makers in the National Museum of Wales which might be helpful. So to start with Britten first.

His list appeared in 1894 in the first edition of *Former Clock and Watch Makers and their Work*. F. J. Britten died in 1913 and the 1919 edition was edited by his son, as was the sixth edition, 1932 (reputedly the best); my copy of this is the current reprint of 1971. It is important to read carefully the introduction to Britten's list. Originally the names were those he knew of or could trace through the records of the Clockmakers' Company. In the early editions he confined himself to London makers, but by the sixth edition he had reached 12,000 names. Quite a few of his names reach to 1894, but from 1830 to this date he made exclusions on various grounds, e.g., if they were still in business. It is important to search Britten in looking for an elusive name but to remember that if the maker was not a member of the Company he may well not be found.

G. H. Baillie's *Watchmakers and Clockmakers of the World* contains 36,000 names and is, of course, the collector's Bible. Like the Bible, however, it must be read with care and a great deal of background knowledge. Many a collector has been very cast down because he cannot trace the name of his man therein. Reciprocally many a dealer has been "made up" when the name on the back plate or top plate is "in the book". However, there is much more to it than that. To understand the lines that Baillie followed in his researches it is imperative to read the prefaces, conventions and addenda carefully. The first edition was published in 1929, the second in 1947 and the third (the edition used here) in 1951; the author is not now living. In regard to English makers it might be thought that Baillie supplemented Britten's list, but in fact in his industry he went right back to the minute-books of the Clockmakers' Company, which were complete from 1632. Volume 2 of Baillie, with an additional 35,000 names was published in 1978, too late to have been used when writing this book.

There are three important provisos to bear in mind when referring to Baillie's book. To quote: "The list extends up to 1825, but a few later makers of distinction have been mentioned. After that date there were too many calling themselves watch and clockmakers who were more merchants than craftsmen." Secondly, not all watchmakers who had served a due apprenticeship and were reputable craftsmen proceeded to membership of the Company. There would be a high percentage of London men and possibly a much lower proportion of provincial and country makers. Thirdly, the dates given are those when they were in contact with the Company or mentioned in the minutes. Some might join late or drop out early. It would seem mistakenly from the short span of many of the entries that their working life was very short and that many died very young. Of course, in other instances we have the full date of birth, apprenticeship, election date and death. The point is that one is often faced with a movement made by a man outside the dates given in Baillie. There could be several reasons for this, but the most likely is that the span listed should not be taken as the extent of a man's full working life. When only one date is mentioned one feels freer to speculate either side of it. It must also be remembered that some makers were "Free of other Companies and Guilds" and would not seek admission to the Clockmakers' Company.

Baillie's third limitation was a self-imposed one, arising in part from the sheer length of the lists. It was that he would not include "makers" whom he judged on evidence as having added little to the watch other than name. How he drew this very difficult distinction it would be hard to say, but this is probably the answer to the many omissions of the names of men whose work has survived to reach the hands of today's collector. As making became more of a manufacture during the nineteenth century, and as the lever emerged as the best escapement, the scope for innovation and invention lessened. The number of craftsmen able to make any outstanding contribution became fewer. This explains the sudden cessation of interest by horologists by the magic date of 1830 and Baillie's curtailment of his list in 1825. The selection of some names and the omission of others, however, raises a big question which is not answered in the current texts: Who in fact can rightly claim to have made the watch on which a name is engraved? It is worth giving a little consideration to this.

The Name on the Watch

Because watchmaking is necessarily a highly skilled process it calls for many different skills and a number of experts in them. Except in the very early crude days no one man could hope to make a watch from beginning to end. It would not be economic for him to do so nor would it be possible for him to serve apprenticeships in all the specialities. A prosperous watchmaker might be able to collect a good team in his workshop but he would need a large and steady amount of work to employ fully every specialist he needed under one roof. Necessarily, then, the "maker" was a co-ordinator, a director and, above all, a finisher. The watches we handle have therefore been made in several different ways. At one end of the range we have the American factory system in which all the tradesmen were assembled in one place and the work very skilfully organized so that the raw materials went in one end and the cased watch came out at the other. The Swiss, more successfully, modified this by having factories making the finished components in specialist factories and assembling them in another factory. This was more efficient and more economic. In this country the Coventry field managed mass production in much smaller quantities rather on the Swiss lines of co-ordinating small workshops. The Lancashire men remained on cottage industry lines for nearly three hundred years until they entered the factory of the Lancashire Watch Company in the 1890s. Under this system the movement or batch of movements was carried by hand from one cottage workshop to the next until "rough" movement had reached a stage where it could be again carried to the finishers in the neighbouring towns (principally Liverpool). No doubt the Clerkenwell workers followed much the same methods. Though highly inefficient administratively, Prescot held most of the English trade until the rise of the Midlands. Yet I have only come across one movement engraved with the name of a Prescot maker—this was Thomas Hornby of Prescot. (Baillie lists a Thos. Hornby of Liverpool who might be the same man.) The Prescot suppliers of the basic movements can sometimes be identified by marks under the dial. It must remain highly significant that the greater portion of the work of building a movement was done by people who, perhaps purposely, were kept well in the background.

It is worth looking at the trades and tradesmen involved in the total process and making two lists. These will almost certainly be incomplete.

The ébauche, "grey" or "rough" movement	*The finished watch*
Plate and pillar maker	Plate gilder
Wheel cutter	Engraver
Pinion fitter	Wheel burnisher
Spring and barrel maker	Hand maker
Chain maker	Dial writer
Hairspring and balance maker	Key maker
Hole jeweller	Finisher
Dial maker	Adjuster
Balance cock maker	Casemaker
Fusee maker	Salesman or shopman
Assembler	

Perhaps the lists balance out roughly in skill, for it will be understood that the rough movement having been designed and made to the "maker's" instructions, had to be taken all down and rebuilt to a high standard of finish when it came into his hands. As set out in the two lists it was a fair division of labour, and if the game was played on these lines it would be reasonable to accept the convention of the second man signing the movement. However, the nearer the division came to the finished article the less claim the signatory had to the title of maker, until at last the watch came virtually or actually from a wholesaler to be retailed. This was the problem facing Baillie in making his list and one is not surprised that by 1825 he was coming across so much evidence of trading and retailing that he felt that it was time to stop compiling. He made a decision of principle, but it did leave a gap of a hundred years, the post-1830 period now of such importance to collectors. If, on the other hand, one consults Britten (sixth edition, 1932) it will be seen that he makes a real attempt to list makers or "makers" into the twentieth century. This is encouraging but experience of using Britten's list, even though it covers a period reaching almost to the end of the pocket watch era, shows that it is not in any way as full and exhaustive as that of Baillie.

Perhaps the best comment comes from Eric Bruton in *Clock Collecting* (1974):

> There are many names not in "Baillie", and this at times upsets dealers and owners. The reason may have been, and sometimes is known to have been, because Baillie did not come across the maker. Most omitted names were excluded deliberately, however. It was common in the latter 18th and 19th century for the name of the retailer (who still called himself a "clockmaker") to be engraved or painted on the dial and often engraved on the brass back plate of the movement. The practice was so common that Baillie deliberately suppressed many names he thought to be those of retailers. Clockmaking factories in London and Birmingham during the period engraved or painted on a "maker's" name as normal practice. Records of Thwaites and Reed of Clerkenwell in possession of the Worshipful Company of Clockmakers even list many famous genuine makers to whom they supplied clock movements in this way. The famous makers supplied factory made clocks on their "cheap lines" in the eighteenth century.

Bruton is speaking of clocks, of course, but with little variation he could say the same thing about watches. This is illustrated in *The Craft of the Clockmaker* by E. J. Tyler. He shows a photograph of a batch of six unfinished watch movements of classical seventeenth-century type (dated about 1670). "They are all alike and show that bulk production was being carried out even at this early date." On similar lines, I have a group of five "rough" Prescot movements (nineteenth-century) fully assembled and ready for the finisher.

One of the results of the "gold rush" of the early 1930s is that we are left with only the movement in many instances. Indeed these are lucky to have survived, for the majority were probably scrapped in the days when people could see no future value in them. Without a hallmark and signed by a name of which there may be no record only a guess can be made about the possible date. A collector should, therefore, never overlook an opportunity of making notes about the dated watches in museum collections. On more than one occasion it has been possible to give a date to one of my movements by seeing a cased watch by the same maker. As far as Lancashire and Liverpool makers are concerned it is very unfortunate that the Liverpool Museum was destroyed by bombing in the blitz of May 1941. However, it was possible by combining the City Museum material with my own to produce a short list of names which do not appear either in Britten or Baillie, together with a date where possible. This has now been done by Brian Loomes in his *Lancashire Clocks and Clockmakers* (1975). This list includes many who were specified as watchmakers only.

20

Restoring a Watch

I WAS interested to find quite early in my watch collecting that though hunting for them was fun, and working through the provenance and mechanism rewarding, the real finish to the whole affair was seeing them restored to their original state and efficiency. So it came about that all the watches in my collection are in full working order. True, their accuracy may not be very high; but then it may never have been much higher in the days when the watches themselves were in their youth. After all there is nothing, to me, so dead as a clock or watch that has been put on one side because it can only limp along or will not go at all. They are interesting but fossilized. Most levers can, in fact, reach a stage when they can be carried in the pocket and be rated as daily timekeepers as satisfactory as the good wristlet. If this seems over-optimistic, it is based on my own experience with a large collection of watches. Even so, it is remarkable that examples made two hundred or more years ago, and with probably a long working life, can be brought back to a condition comparable to their state when new. Of course, a few had to be sold out as scrap when there was some major problem such as broken balance staff or irreplaceable mainspring; but naturally one tried to avoid making such a buying mistake as that.

The watches we now come by have nearly all had a long working life and had been laid aside often because they were thought to be irreparable or at any rate not worth repair. Sometimes, of course, they stopped being used when they became unfashionable or the owner died. In any case a good deal of wear is inevitable. However, to balance this, they were not built as things are now with a view to obsolescence. The purchase of a watch was a once-for-all exercise. It was expected to last the owner his lifetime and be fit to be passed on to the next generation or generations. Repeated repair, particularly in the verges, was allowed for, and this was simple enough. Though we usually know the birthday of our watch, we can only guess the length of time it was in use. As an example of long use, my oldest watch, which is single cased, had lived in the pocket so long that two holes had been worn in the back and these had to be repaired. Watches, both ancient and modern, never have sufficient maintenance, and though this might lead to increased wear, it might equally lead to their being discarded simply for this reason. So often one can find a watch in which the balance is moving in a tired worn-out way and looking quite done for. But after the removal of years of dirt, some minor adjustment, and the provision of fresh oil, it will come back from the watchmaker as brisk as when it was first made.

Among the difficulties of reinstatement is that of obtaining new parts. The material service for the modern wrist watch is highly organized on Swiss lines and almost everything except the obsolete can be obtained by quoting the part number. When pocket watches were in vogue there was similar efficiency, certainly for the factory-made types and possibly back into the last century. All spare material of this kind has now been used up and the only source is by cannibalization. For this reason the collector should collect movements as well as cased watches whenever he has a chance. Naturally, the further back one goes in time the less the standardization and interchangeability. Having a new part made is hardly feasible today, for not only are few watchmakers able to do this but fewer still are willing to spend the time. It is a matter of a good deal of persuasion and no little money to have a simple balance staff cut and to have a new cylinder turned is many times more difficult. Advertisements are carried in *Antiquarian Horology* of firms who are able to restore any watch. Necessarily, however, this calls for many hours of an expert's time. Such repairs cannot be other than costly and justified only for a really important piece. In short the organizing of the repair service has a high priority for the collector.

The shortage of properly trained and experienced watch repairers has come about in this country alongside the extinction of watchmaking itself. It is primarily due, however, to the fact that apprentices have long ago ceased to be attracted into a trade which is not only very exacting but also has never been properly paid. There are many tradesmen who have opted for more regular and better-paid jobs. It is, in fact, very difficult to earn a proper living in repairing. So often the craftsman is asked to spend a lot of time on a movement which does not justify the expense by a customer who cannot afford a proper fee. This is a curious and vicious circle which does not match the wages earned by quite unskilled work today. Another point is that many of the problems met with in older watches are the result of short cuts taken by previous repairers either to save time or cover lack of skill. These have all to be undone and re-done. Many of the so-called repairers today have had no proper training and are known in the trade as "cowboys". Largely they copy the motor mechanic and are able (in wrist watches, of course) to remove the faulty part and replace it by new material. This cannot be of any help to the collector. He will be better in the hands of a skilled, possibly amateur, engineer who can handle a watchmaker's lathe and be able to fashion a part by copying it (always supposing the part is not missing!).

At this stage the collector has to consider to what extent he should train himself to be his own repairer. As a minimum he should be able to handle the superficial matters. He should learn how to take movements out of the cases, i.e., something about case screws, sleeves, and hinges in the older movements. At this stage it will then be possible to decide at least roughly what is at fault and what needs doing. Next he should practise removal and replacement of the hands or the dial. Then on an unimportant movement he should practise removal of the balance and the more difficult replacement. To get as far as this calls for a simple kit of tools (see illustration No. 119), which can be bought from local or postal firms. Whether he should go further than this on his own is the crucial point. To take down a clock movement and reassemble it is quite a different matter in comparison to working on the much smaller watch. One alternative is to put the intact movement through a cleaning machine and then simply re-oil, providing that there is nothing seriously wrong with it. Indeed this is simply all that is done by many repairing firms. There is, however, plenty of evidence to show that, given a steady hand and mechanical aptitude, the ordinary person can learn to strip a movement right down (always remember to take the power off the mainspring), clean it, re-oil and rebuild. Actual repairing is, of course, something more. It is unlikely that it will be possible to find anybody to give him personal tuition but luckily it is all in the books for the amateur. These are listed in the Chapter 24, though often out of print today. Books such as Britten's *Watch and Clockmaker's Handbook* (1884 and subsequent editions) can be turned up in the public libraries and details studied. Britten has the advantage of covering the older watches. Donald de Carle's *Practical Watch Repairing* (3rd edition, 1969) is still available. Necessarily this is orientated to today's wrist watches but there is a chapter on the English lever ("which really needs a book to itself"). However, all the basics are very fully covered—tools, methods, turning, timing, etc.—and with this manual at hand and well thumbed the collector could if he wished turn himself into a practical repairer of his own watches, thus adding a most rewarding angle to his hobby.

To do this would call for not only much patient work but a very great deal of time. Even if this were invested one would still lack the watchmaker's long experience and expertise. Looking at the position in the early stages it seemed to me, and still does, that the best plan was to search for a watchmaker well grounded in yesterday's watches. Many firms were tried and investigated and many enquiries made until finally a craftsman emerged. Very competently he restored my relatively modern watches and returned them without delay. (An important point this, because the good watchmakers are working against a backlog of repairs; they are not short of work, the difficulty is to make it pay.) Admittedly his face would fall at some of the wrecks brought in, but he mastered them all. However, there was an age limit to what he was prepared to do (except as far as clocks were concerned) and he had for business reasons to turn down fusees and verges. The search had now to begin again.

As a result I found my friend Mr. R. E. Phillips. He was traced by his R.E.P. monogram appearing on work coming down from a small firm for whom he was working after retiring from his own business. By this time he had finally given up working "for the trade", but when approached he was pleased to have an opportunity to take on my watches at his leisure and so keep his craft in being. Mr. Phillips was born in 1900 and his apprenticeship was interrupted by service in the First World War, but he continued at watchmaking afterwards and subsequently gained his certificate as a Craft Member of the British Horological Institute by examination. Every week I call on him, carrying the current watch, and we discuss the problems found in the last watch and how he managed to get round them. Very rarely is he beaten and I take into my hand a specimen moving briskly and rated to exact time in nearly every case. His success is not only due to his long basic experience and awareness of what the previous repairer has done but also to his determination. In this he is helped by the fact that when he comes to an impasse he can, in his leisure, get down from his bench, hang up his apron, and wait for the inspiration of the morning. Perhaps the most remarkable thing about Mr. Phillips is that having started in 1914 he is, like my previous watchmaker, fully versed in the vagaries of the going barrel lever movement. These he takes in his stride. In his working life, however, he was, as can be calculated, never called upon to deal with fusees or verges or, indeed, rarer escapements. Such is his basic skill, however, that even when over seventy he was able to train himself to deal with them successfully.

This happy association with Mr. Phillips is, of course, the basis for my view that most old watches can be persuaded to return to work. There was much more to it than that though, for I have had the privilege of sitting each week at a fount of knowledge. It was a continued unconscious education and most of any merit this book may have is largely due to my tutor. Possibly in some ways it was a drawback, for why should I try to learn to repair when it could be done so imaginatively by someone else? Other collectors may not be so lucky in finding someone to refurbish their watches. I mention my own experience in some detail, however, to point out the benefit of searching diligently for expert help. It is easier to find the craftsman than it is for him to find time to do the work. It is not to be thought that Mr. Phillips was always happy when he saw the problems and the botching in some of my triumphant finds. To make him rub his hands it had to be a high-class movement or, better still, a good clock.

It is just possible that the keen learner may come across a tradesman who might be prepared to give him some tuition. This is not easy, for several reasons, but provided that the pupil is prepared to read the books and do a great deal of work at home, the plan might work. It is, however, very difficult indeed to share the expertise which results from a long apprenticeship and many years of experience. Even in the much cruder field of the clock the amateur remains baffled by the "mystery". For instance, it is not terribly difficult to make a replacement brass-faced pendulum which looks as good as the original. When it comes, however, to such questions as the strength of the suspension spring, the weight of the bob, or even the best length, the only information lies in the expertise of the craftsman. In the watch movement the points are even finer and more vital to the final satisfactory running.

Another approach is to be found in night-school classes, even though this may necessitate a journey if there are none locally. In my home area we have been fortunate in being able to attend a Clockwork Class each week for the last few years, run by an enthusiastic craftsman whose family have been watchmakers for generations. Usually we set out with an old clock which has been built well enough to be worth restoring, and working both at home and in class we recreate something that is very much appreciated today. The class has recently started the new session with over twenty pupils, indicating the interest there is in the hobby of repairing clocks and watches. For young people who want to take up the matter seriously, it is not now possible for them to find watchmakers who could accept them as apprentices nor could they afford to serve their time in the old-fashioned way. The British Horological Institution has, however, set up training schemes at various technical colleges where the theory and practice can be learned. The length of these courses varies but may last up to three or four years. This is excellent but, of course, sadly belated when we recall the Swiss training schools in being for at least a hundred and fifty years.

Whatever steps the amateur takes to learn or teach himself clock and watch restoration, he should not, in my view, tackle expensive or antique pieces. It is so easy to ruin a clock case by over-enthusiasm, to lose or break a watch part. With this proviso there can be no doubt that many people can learn to become reasonably competent watch repairers with the more modern wrist and pocket watches. It must be remembered, however, that it is essential to be very much better than the current "cowboys" of the repairing trade.

21
Collecting Watches

THERE are risks and dangers in all kinds of collecting, the main one being that of spending too much time, money and interest in one narrow field. This is accentuated as far as watches are concerned because there are very few local societies and on the whole the collector is on his own. It is difficult indeed to find a local watchmaker who can handle the older watch and rare to meet anybody to discuss them. Such people are to be found but they need to be traced and coaxed out of their back rooms. Even in London the circulation is not good and we remain a collection of individuals who are loath to advertise themselves in view of the increasing risks to their collections from burglary. There is, therefore, no kind of organized market from which to choose as there is for instance in coins, stamps, books and so on. There is no weekly magazine, there are no dealers' lists, and very few advertisments. The *Horological Journal* and *Antiquarian Horology* are not exactly angled towards the modest learner or tyro in the field. While it is obviously advisable for him to have an academic and technical grasp of the subject, even possibly some historical and biographical interest, there is a wide gap between this approach and the practicalities of building a collection. The gap, is of course, a financial one. The collector of the past was both a cultured and a wealthy man. Today there are many more people who would like to indulge their acquisitive and artistic ideas on an ordinary income. It is for these that this book is principally designed.

How this can be done is a problem of two dimensions. The first is scarcity of material. Relatively speaking only a very limited number of watches were made in the antique period of the seventeenth and eighteenth centuries. Hence the idea, fostered in most texts, that horology flourished only in the pre-1830 era. It follows that pieces from these years will be rare and may be prohibitive in price for the ordinary man. Following 1830, for the next century the output steadily increased, though possession was always limited by the potential owner's income. There is still a relatively large supply of watches made during the last hundred and fifty years though their cost, like everything else, is rising. It is interesting to note that this rise was only seen during the last ten or fifteen years. Before this it was possible, for instance, to buy a reasonable silver verge for about £5. The same piece would today sell for about £50. Apart, however, from rising prices and inflation there is an added factor—that of Value Added Tax. It can be seen that the dealer (when he allows for overheads and profit) has to ask the buyer at least 50 per cent more than his buying price. Another angle of V.A.T. is that in order to cut down this 50 per cent "mark up" the dealer has to offer less to a selling customer than he would like. The morass of V.A.T. is very difficult for the collector; the only fact that emerges is that, come what may, the buyer has to pay up. In some trades the tax is only on the dealer's "mark-up", whereas here it is on the total cost (antique pieces possibly only on the "mark-up"). The first factor of scarcity compounded with the second factor of real and artificial rise faces the would-be collector.

It goes without saying that, having posed this economic problem, I have (like the economists) no practical answer to it. Let us instead pass on to the possible methods of finding watches. The prestige London auction rooms issue priced lists after their sales. These are reproduced in *Antiquarian Horology*, but it need not be stressed that price levels are discouraging to all but the serious investor. At local auctions one may come upon interesting clocks but rarely watches. The important ones are channelled to London and the more ordinary find their way into the hands of specialized dealers. Advertisements are rare: a few will be found in *Exchange and Mart*. Watches are, however, on the whole rather too tricky to buy by post without personal inspection. In practice then one is left with only two sources. It may be possible to strike up a working arrangement with a dealer or dealers who understand watches sufficiently to be confident in handling them. Presumably the dealers' supply source is the "knocker" who traditionally works his way from house to house buying, as it were, on the doorstep. From the dealer, possibly passing through several dealers, the watch finds its way to the second field, that of the antique shop. The owner of the shop has a second source of supply, that of clients and owners who sell items to him over the counter, and perhaps a third if he buys in the more professional local salerooms. It is important to realize exactly what seam is being worked in all these involved transactions. It is, of course, leaving on one side the occasional dispersal of some small collection, that of the family heirloom or grandfather's watch. This is the minor or major treasure that has been lying in the drawer or in the bank for generations, the oil drying and congealing and the dust accumulating and the sentiment attached to it evaporating. Incidentally such a watch may be persuaded to run again if it warmed in a sympathetic female hand or bosom for half an hour or so!

Thus the watch finally appears in the shop window, possibly after having passed through several hands to which a little profit has stuck, until it has reached a price level at which any further profit can only be made by retail sale to the public. If, on the other hand, it has been bought over the counter shrewdly, then the customer may reap some of this benefit in a business run on the basis of small profits on quick returns. Shops differ in their policy. Some, often the long-established and reliable firms, will tag the correct market price and be prepared to wait, whatever the buying price may have been, but this means, they have to tie up money in stock for an indefinite period, not a happy situation during inflation. The buyer will learn to assess each situation as time goes on. If, however, he gains a reputation as a genuine collector (and not an amateur dealer) he will find a good deal of accommodation as to actual price. Now, praise be, there are always plenty of antique shops, either locally or in nearby towns or farther afield when on holiday. It is, in my experience, a matter of seeking them all out and making regular tours. Armchair methods will not work and promises to "let you know" are difficult to keep. There is a keen demand and more than once regular visiting has produced items that have never even reached the window.

It may be thought that my policy of simply buying in competition with everybody else (many of whom are interested only in owning a single watch is very unenterprising; that there should be some possibility of entering the market at an earlier stage such as buying from other collectors or amateur salesmen. This I have not found easy or reliable. Shopping has its advantages in that most of the available watches do find their way there—and the occasional visit to the London circuit will show this very clearly. A shop also has its reputation to consider and is anxious that there should be a satisfied customer and a future client. Even when buying a watch as it stands one has far better protection in a shop than outside. It is, however, necessary to understand the proprietor's position apart from his inability to give much of a guarantee.

When the sale has been satisfactorily concluded the buyer has an item of a known and probably fair retail value. If shortly afterwards the collector changes his mind, he finds that he owns a piece of much less value, i.e., the price at which the watch was originally brought into stock. Unless there is a specific agreement he cannot expect to get his money back in the original shop or any other. For the proprietor has to set to and make another sale (and pay another dose of v.a.t.). This is a hard fact of collecting seldom fully enough appreciated. It can reasonably be hoped that the piece, sooner or (more likely) later, will appreciate. Thus it underlines the rule that a collector must be genuine and not be misled into thinking that he can be a dealer as well. Basically a dealer should not collect unless he is re-investing his profits and a collector must almost never deal. They must remain on opposite sides of the fence even though each is dependent on the other, and one should never begrudge a dealer his fair profit. A collection of anything old or antique is quite sound financially in the long term, but it is far from being a means of making money and should never be looked upon as such. Watches are obviously appreciating but, of course, they will only do so provided people have the money to buy them and the inclination to do so. This is a simple rule in any market.

In buying a watch, then, the important criterion is to see that the price is a fair one. This can only be assessed by experience in comparing the price range in other shops. My experience is that dealers and proprietors have a surprisingly uniform sense of value but occasionally prices do obtain in shops catering for the people who are looking for something old rather than collecting. Of course, when faced with something unique and unlikely to be met with again it may be a pleasure to "pay over the odds". The second criterion is a matter of expertise—the appearance and the mechanical state. Often this can only be a matter of a relatively quick examination on the counter but it should be as prolonged as possible. The watch may have been overhauled, it may run when wound with the Birch key. If it does so then it is unlikely that there are many parts missing. The type of escapement, the period, the hallmark can all be checked. Usually my friends in the trade will let me take the watch home on approval. Here one can consult the books, see what the faults are, take a second opinion and think about purchase. The appearance, i.e., the scars of many years, need careful assessment, since there is a world of difference between a watch which has been little and carefully used and one which has had very hard wear. Some of these points have been made before but the importance now is a question of how far the attractiveness of the watch can be restored, of how much needs to be, and can be, done to reinstate it to something like its pristine condition. Bearing in mind that case repairers are rare, one does not want to assemble a lot of battered old cases.

First of all, is everything present—the bow and bezel in particular. If the case is rolled gold one looks at the warranty in years and signs of wearing through—such wear cannot be dealt with. Gilt watch cases can be regilded. Then there are the catches. In a verge the button may be worn through or lost, or the catch itself missing. In a hunting case the flap should open on pressure and shut with a click. The inner glass (crystal) of a hunter is often missing and not easy to replace. In a key-wound watch the back should open on pressure of the push-piece and again shut tight. Then there is the question of the glass in an open-faced watch. It is unwise to by a verge without a glass or one which is badly scratched or cracked, since a new one will take a great deal of finding. If the dial is very obiously cracked or chipped this very much detracts from the appearance unless, as in a machine-made watch, it can be exchanged for something better.

It is by no means easy to rewrite a watch dial when some of the numerals are worn. As for the hands, they should if possible be original or at least congruous. If broken or missing, except in the case of a relatively modern watch, new hands may have to be fashioned.

In gold cases one would check that all the parts were properly hallmarked. Some recent cases do not carry a dome (to save cost in manufacture); others are very flimsy for the same reason. No doubt thin cases are just as effective as thick, but it is as well to try to flex the back or the dome to know exactly what one is buying. Knocks and scars on the case are obvious and lower the value. In the machine-made case it is important to see that sleeve action for hand-setting is working, for new parts are hard to find. One of the common omissions is to buy a watch (or clock) and forget to ask for a key. One could amplify this checklist even further until it might appear that no timepiece should be bought with any defect whatsoever. Obviously this cannot be practical: what is important is not to find after purchase that the piece is irreparable because of some vital defect. As has been noted previously, and this may be an unjustifiable personal idiosyncrasy, I feel that a watch has much less attraction if it cannot be restored to some kind of going order.

The actual reinstatement has been dealt with in a separate chapter, but the mere acquisition of a further item is not the end of the matter for a collector. Since watches are small enough to be easily mislaid, lost, stolen, or confused with others, it is necessary to catalogue them. Each must be given a serial number and a tie-on miniature label which can also carry a summary. It is then necessary to build up some system whereby all the information relative to the piece can be retrieved when the watch itself is not on hand. The great thing is to record everything at an early date so that it will not be forgotten with the passing of time and the building up of the collection. Such matters as where it was found, what was its cost, what repairs were needed, who carried them out and with what result, together with what has been found from research and how this is related to other known examples. My own system is rather elaborate and most collectors will settle for something simpler. It involves a serial number carried with salient details on a tag label, an index card giving a fuller summary and filed according to type and escapement, a loose-leaf binder in numerical sequence containing all the details, and finally lists of each type of escapement for comparison. Despite all this there will still be occasions when a watch proves impossible to trace because it has been scrapped, given away or part-exchanged and no final note of disposal made. Not to mention the possibility of two watches being given the same serial number. My experience is that unless good records are kept (as an alternative to what may seem to be a good memory) great confusion will result during the years of collecting.

Photography can be a great help and it was because of this that I bought a good camera and set up a dark-room. Apart from being of possible use to the police, photographs enable one to show and discuss the watch *in absentia*, as it were. Providing that the pictures are realistic enough, then they are the only practical and safe way of exhibiting one's collection. To have a photograph of each watch is, of course, a tremendous help to any filing system. Actually the everyday undecorated watch is not highly photogenic, being simply a disc of varying thickness and curvature. Moreover, since the cases are either of silver or gold, there is little variation to reward the use of colour, though the correct choice of background helps considerably. My personal efforts have entirely been in the field of black-and-white because the amateur can do the essential enlarging himself. For the non-professional, colour processsing is hardly practical yet. My method very briefly is to fix my camera in the tripod stand using a lens extension for close work. Exact focussing, lighting (I use daylight), positioning to mitigate reflections from the movement and case, have all to be learnt from hard experience. Someone who is already a competent photographer should easily overcome these problems, but even he must remember to set the hands to a position in which they do not obscure other detail. If the watch glass is domed to any extent it will have to be opened to get any reasonable picture of the dial. Of course, photography calls for a lot of time and the results have to be good if it is to be worthwhile, but without it the collector will be short of his full reward.

Finally there is what the Administration would refer to as "security". From early times owners have lost their watches to pickpockets, muggers and highwaymen, and the old news-sheets carried advertisements offering rewards. Today, when the value and the scarcity of these same watches is rising, it is the collector who is the target and *Antiquarian Horology* regularly carries a Police Page (or pages) referring to thefts of clocks. Clearly there is no difficulty in disposing of outstanding examples and the same practice no doubt extends to watches. Museums go to the extent of stencilling or engraving their number on watch movements. These items are unlikely to change hands but collectors would be loath to brand privately owned examples. Private houses are increasingly broken into, sometimes by specialists who know exactly the value of antiques, Insurance companies are reluctant to insure collections kept at home, and if they do so, insist on a great deal of burglarproofing. I have no hesitation in keeping everything of any value in the bank. My bank charges a small annual fee for this, but makes it clear that though the same high standard of security is given to the deposit as they give to their own valuables there is no insurance cover. For less valuable articles at home a locked steel filing cabinet is as good as anything—a safe will attract (and yield to) skilled attention.

It is unfortunate that collections of anything portable or even movable—stamps, coins, clocks, old silver, paintings or even simply cash—are at risk in the home today. The corollary of collecting is exhibition, but this is largely impossible now; indeed it is unwise to let it be known that one collects. Even a little display cabinet in the lounge, showing a few choice pieces, would be too much of an attraction to either an amateur or professional burglar. Writers about their hobby run a particular risk.

22

The Massacre of the Watches

WHATEVER a collector may happen to be interested in he is always liable to be harrowed by stories of the treasures that he has missed: the "if onlys"—"if only you had been in last week, last month, last year . . .". One learns to discount the might-have-been. What has interested me much more in regard to pocket watches has been the tales of watch wrecking and scrapping, and in particular the biscuit-boxes full of ticking movements under the counters of dealers and jewellers. Since on my collecting rounds the same story was repeated in identical terms by different witnesses, the evidence had some circumstantial weight—even allowing for the inevitable exaggeration. When compiling the lists of Lancashire watchmakers the negative support for these tales became obvious. There were hundreds or thousands of watch finishers in the area based on the busy movement makers of Prescot. Each finisher must have made and signed some hundreds of watches in his lifetime. Not only that, but there was to be considered the very much larger London trade and the lesser Coventry trade. In looking at the survival rate of this large output of watches it seemed surprisingly small, particularly since those that had survived to come into my collection, for instance, were intact and robust. Clearly there would have been a natural wastage over the years but this did not convincingly explain the scarcity of today. Baillie, who scoured the public and private collections between 1929 and 1951, frequently had to be satisfied by a single example to identify a maker. The Lancashire museums similarly show single specimens only of the many names, and more usually cannot show anything at all, even a single movement of well-established makers. In the same way, my own collection has few duplicated names and many wide gaps.

This negative evidence, the many blanks in survival, fits completely with the stories of widespread destruction, so that the collector now is quite rightly elated by his occasional discovery. It is almost certainly not due to the fact that large numbers of watches are hidden away in collections. Such collections, made at an earlier date, are most likely to consist of prestige makers, decorative gems and complicated pieces which would have escaped destruction. We have to remember that until recent years very few people were interested in watches. Until the publication of Clutton and Daniels in 1965 we only had the successive editions of Britten, Baillie's *Watches* in 1929 and Camerer Cuss's *The Story of Watches* in 1952. All the other books on watches in this country have been published since 1965. While the massacre was being carried out those who were doing it were not aware that they were vandalizing a heritage. They hardly knew the significance or history of the various types of movements or watches they scrapped. Nor, significantly, did they or anybody else greatly care. It might be added that as far as my reading goes nobody has even yet published the fact that it *has* occurred. No doubt horologists are aware of what went on but have never spoken of it. Of course, watches are still being scrapped today because of the very high price of gold bullion, but this is confined to the modern watch of no present antique value. The only parallel collective vandalism which occurs to me is the melting down of pre-1922 British silver coins which in later years will throw up a similar dearth for collectors.

The basis for this wave of destruction, which extended to gold jewellery of the heavy Victorian type, was the value of the gold watch case. Since the best movements rated such cases, these suffered most. Silver cased watches probably largely escaped, they will predominate in present collections. It seems, though there can be no proof of this, that the wave may have started for patriotic reasons in the First World War. Gold was needed for the war effort and the proceeds may have gone into Victory Bonds, but once started, the momentum continued through the difficult post-war 1920s. When this country went off the gold standard in 1930 the bullion price increased, and at about the same time men were abandoning the pocket watch for the wrist watch. As a result many watches were scrapped and though, no doubt, many of these were modern watches the older heirlooms and antiques were swept into the pot. Thus the story of one dealer having a stock of ten thousand Waltham movements.

We now reach the stage of the tales of biscuit-tins, butter-boxes, sacks and tea-chests full of movements of all kinds. It was of this time that my friend Stanley Smith would tell me about his lunchtime searches through the boxes under the counter. At the price of sixpence each he built up a collection of the finest antique movements. Mr. R. E. Phillips gives me an independent description of what was happening in Liverpool in the 1920s and remembers well the shops who specialized in scrapping. Today he reproaches himself that he could not see far enough ahead to understand what was being lost, and only kept a few examples himself. However, his wages as an employed watchmaker were so low that he needed every penny, in addition to having to scrape a few more by working at home on repairs most evenings. What was going on in Liverpool was happening on a similar scale in jewellers' shops and pawnbrokers throughout the country.

Perhaps it is not too much to say that millions of uncased movements of all vintages resulted. Had they survived it would have been a different story for horology, but their sheer bulk made this impossible even though a biscuit-tin would contain about two hundred of them. Their market value *en masse* was between threepence and sixpence whether old or new. At this price they would be bought by watch repairers as a source of spares when new parts would be expensive or unobtainable. Largely this would only apply to modern watches with interchangeability though, of course, as the pocket watch was going out of fashion this use would be running down. The movements would be of very little value to the scrap metal merchant who would be reluctant to buy them. Many of the hoards simply ended up on the rubbish dump or were thrown into the canal. Some of the older specimens had some intrinsic gold, in the shape of gold hands, gold balances and gold dials, which were well worth picking out. Then there is the gouhlish business of mutilating verges for their ornate and delicately designed and executed watch cocks for use as jewellery. Mary Flower, in her standard work *Jewellery* (1968), notes this as a short-lived phase of fashion from about 1885 onwards. She condemns it as in the worst taste and regards those who did it as vandals. Britten (1932 edition) remarks, "A few years ago a taste for watch cock necklaces, brooches and bracelets arose, and thousands of interesting movements were destroyed in mad haste to supply material for an evanescent fancy". The one example that came under my notice contained thirty cocks. There are apparently still some collectors who amass these parts and encourage mutilation. As far as the "gold rush" was concerned the verge cocks do not appear to have been specially salvaged, though one Manchester firm is reported to have done this. It was also possible to show a commercial return when costs were lower by burning consignments on the open hearth to recover the gold used in gilding by the mercury process.

One of the most reliable witnesses to the scale of destruction is my friend, Dr. Denis Chapman, of the Liverpool University School of Business Studies. His particular interest is industrial archaeology, with horology as a hobby. Dr. Chapman was friendly with Professor D. S. Torrens, the noted horologist of Trinity College, Dublin. The Professor was in the habit of making collecting forays to this country in search of old watch-making machinery and movements in the 1930s and 1940s. Liverpool was only one of his hunting grounds—London and Coventry were also visited. When Liverpool was the venue the two would team up and, hiring a taxi, would tour the pawnbrokers with which Liverpool was richly endowed. The Professor was expected and the interesting movements had been kept on one side for him. He would return to Dublin with a heavy bag of treasures. He must have been one of the few working on the side of the angels to save the victims of the massacre. Mr. Charles Allix tells me that Professor Torrens built up a great body of knowledge from the dissection of his specimens. This was communicated in various published papers but, unfortunately, it was never brought together in one definitive book. Professor Torrens is now with the angels himself and it is not clear what happened to his collection, but wherever it is now it is certain to be encyclopedic in regard to old watchmakers. Pawnbrokers have always had a steady profit in the gold watch trade though, as with jewellers, the market is now running in favour of preserving the intact watch. Another channel of the "watch drain" between the wars was an army of "knockers" who would regularly and systematically comb the towns and villages in search of secondhand gold and do very well from their gold-mining at the expense of the old and the antique watches.

The main witness of the extent of the destruction wrought is a dealer from whom quite a few of my pieces have been bought over the years. It should be said at once that he was not responsible for the initial destruction of the watch cases. However, in the depression year of 1931 he became redundant and though knowing nothing of watches he began to make his living out of the large numbers of discarded movements which had been wrenched out and thrown under the counter. At that time shops had sprung up, the "gold shops", which did nothing but buy old gold, and to them there was a constant stream of customers. This was not so much because the abandonment of the gold standard had caused gold to be worth more, but because of the depression that followed in the wake of the Wall Street crash of 1929. As well as getting his supplies from the local gold shops, jewellers and pawnbrokers, he advertised in the *Pawnbrokers Gazette* for supplies in bulk. Not knowing anything at that time about the movements, both modern and antique were mixed together and he was unaware of anybody who was interested in buying any choice horological pieces. He learned enough to wrench out a gold balance or a gold dial, while watchmakers sold him gold timing studs. He also learned to test for gold and kept it on one side, but the bulk of the movements he stored in strong Dutch butter-boxes. Each would hold forty to fifty pounds of movements. These he sold at ninepence a pound to the smelters who burned them in the open hearth to recover the small amount of gold in the gilding. For this purpose only the English-made movements with a good thickness of gilt were suitable. He does not think that the silver watch cases were ever scrapped in this way, though the heavier ones might have been added to the scrapping of large pieces of plate. By selling four or five boxes a week he was able to earn a reasonable living for that time until the outbreak of World War II when the breaking up of watches settled to normal levels again. However, we can sit back and contemplate the effect on the watch population of disposing of two to three hundred pounds of movements each week by one man alone. There must have been many others engaged on the same ploy.

The main target was the 18ct. watch case and since the crude method of evisceration was simply to twist out the movement by breaking the hinge it follows that such hinged watches were at least nineteenth-century or older. The machine-made watch, of course, had to be unscrewed rather more tediously. On the whole, then, it seems to me that there is quite adequate evidence to show that a very large proportion of gold cased watches were destroyed in the gold rush of the 1920s which rose to a sustained peak in the 1930s. Perhaps it is not too much to say that the majority of heirlooms suffered this fate. It resulted from a mixture of depression and unemployment, cupidity and ignorance. How ironical it was that after watchmaking had collapsed in this country in the early part of this century we should proceed within a few years to smash up so many of the examples of our former eminence in the trade.

23

The Analysis

My collection of pocket watches has illustrated the changes in design over the two most important centuries of its development—say from about 1720 to 1930. Outwardly during this time it has mainly been a small utilitarian object of much less aesthetic appeal than, for instance, bracket clocks or the other highly decorated and much-photographed French clocks. In watches the charm and fascination must lie in the movement and its execution. Usually the progress towards perfection and precision of the movement is written up as a story of remarkable, almost romantic, triumph of technical advance, with the watchmakers as the heroes. I emerge from my study with a somewhat different opinion which naturally is very diffidently advanced. It seems to me that the Englishman and his watchmakers could more correctly be said to have conducted a long and brilliant defence of the *status quo*. Just as we have preserved cricket as a fascinating game from the far-off days when it started on the village green. The rules may have changed a little but the tactics and the strategy remain the same, and "stonewalling" is still in fashion. So all the effort was put into improving the watch within its accepted form. The received form of the movement grew out of the turret clock via the domestic clock to a pattern that was fixed as long ago as the fourteenth or fifteenth century. No one seems to have doubted that this was the best that could be devised and, until the technical advances of very recent years, no one ever thought of any other method of recording portable time.

By the middle of the seventeenth century the watch had evolved on the lines of a small round clock with a sprung balance replacing the pendulum and so fitting it to be carried in the pocket and keep reasonable time. The readout was the traditional dial and hands, the power was a coiled spring, the transmission was by geared trainwork, and the release of power was by escapement. The whole vocabulary was fixed and remains in use today with very few additions. When the pocket watch passed away it was essentially still in this pattern.

Moreover, when the wrist watch took its place the format was unchanged and we use it almost universally to this day, hundreds of years after its inception. Research and change had been narrowly within the limits of the frictional rest set up by the escapement. As far as can be seen no watchmaker questioned the traditional basic layout or made any attempt to break away from it. This is not really surprising, at least in this country, though it is odd that there was not revolt in other countries. Since a charter was granted to the Clockmakers' Company in 1631 a very long apprenticehsip was insisted upon and during this period a young man was indoctrinated into technical conservationism. As he grew into the trade his professional expertise reached such a high level that, except in the early days of watchmaking, amateur and unconventional ideas could find no footing. This is surely the most extreme conservatism. It is paralleled only by the deeply rooted conservatism found in the professions of the Law, the Church and, above all, Medicine.

It is underlined by one of the few engineers who has written about horology, namely Paul M. Chamberlain in his *It's About Time*. A similar attitude emerges from Swinburne's book *The Mechanism of the Watch*, always bearing in mind that by my calculation the author was 92 when he published. Both men were well qualified and experienced engineers. Chamberlain describes every known variation of escapement, and indeed invents one himself, in a book which shows his vast historical research and his own deep horological competence. But having read the book as closely as possible, the negative side seems to me to be striking. Nowhere does he or even Swinburne suggest that the watch could be designed on any other lines to give greater mechanical efficiency or simplicity. Like the watchmakers, they thought exclusively within the limits of the long-accepted watch.

It could be argued that watchmakers were themselves horological engineers but if so they had the drawback of working in a very limited field without any formal training or contact with the wider world of engineering principle or theory. It might also be said that engineers were called in to horology. In the early days they no doubt made the hand-tools and the primitive engines for cutting wheels and pinnions and so on. When watch factories were built, a great deal of engineering genius was used to devise machines that would do quickly and accurately work that was previously done by hand. On analysis, however, all the engineers were doing was to find a better way of building the same watch. They had simply joined the watchmakers in the age-old pursuit of improving the long-accepted movement. One is left with the strong feeling that if at any time during the last hundred years or so an engineer had been asked to design a mechanism to record time he would have come up with some very different methods of providing and transmitting power which would have been mechanically far more efficient. This is, of course, what had to be done, though only in the last few years, when faced with electronics, the tuning fork, the quartz crystal, and so on.

The watch did not, however, live and grow in this sort of liberal climate. By the sheer aristocracy of its craftsmen change and growth only took place within the pattern in which the watch was originally conceived so many centuries ago. The "Art and Mystery" (a name to which watchmaking is in every sense entitled) was a code within which craftsmen developed the most meticulous skills. It was almost a closed religious order, devoted to the improvement but not the replacement of the pattern.

Herein lies the charm of the very practical study of examples from the history of the watch. It is a field in which we can see clearly defined boundaries and work between fixed parameters. There are no politics and little economics; the swings of opinion are gently reasoned discussions and remain so. All the facts can be seen as we hold the old watches in our hands. But to return to the beginning of the book, what is the fascination that the personal timepiece exercises on so many people? It may be that we have been so long its servant that there is a love/hate feeling for the mechanism that programmes our lives. We may foster the old watch in positive rebellion against today's watch, which is accurate to a few seconds a month. Any future based on split-second slavery can hardly be a happy one. We all feel, quite mistakenly, that the more leisurely and less time-conscious life of the past would have been happier, and crave to return to it. Almost certainly the bygone feeling is the large part of the fascination of the old watch. Instead of applauding today's high accuracy we would prefer the leisure of a timetable in which a few minutes either way did not really matter, so that when we can find, restore, and carry round with us a memento of those past times we have, even by so little, an escape from the gloom and unrest of today.

24

Horological Literature

OF equal importance to the collection of watches is the need to read up what has already been written about them, and a collector will want to build up some kind of a library of his own or locate the books in nearby public libraries. The subject and its field is relatively small and well defined. It has also been well researched over the years, particularly in the antique section though much less so in the modern. In the English scene the watchmakers were doers rather than writers and they published very little indeed. Their work has survived to speak for itself. There were no periodicals until the foundation of the British Horological Institute in 1858 but the *Horological Journal* has appeared monthly ever since. *Antiquarian Horology* has been published quarterly since 1953. Britten published the first over-all horological text in this country in 1894, and for many years this remained, in successive editions, the only British publication. Baillie published his *Watches* and *Watchmakers and Clockmakers of the World* in 1929 and Camerer Cuss his *The Story of Watches* in 1952. The next definitive work was *Watches* by Clutton and Daniels in 1965. Since then there has been an increasing number of books of very varying standards. Many of these have been of the "coffee table book" type, extremely attractively produced and illustrated, but of little use to the active collector. It is unfortunate that many, if not most, of the really helpful texts are now out of print and can only be found in the expensive secondhand market. If they are to be found they are well worth buying; occasionally they are reprinted relatively inexpensively.

A recent book, *Watch Collecting* by Kenneth Ullyett (1970), published by Frederick Muller, has an excellent and comprehensive chapter "To the Reader...". Here all the books likely to be of use to the collector are listed and briefly reviewed. I have been able to assemble most of the available books covering the British field and these are set out opposite:

Abbott, Henry G. *History of the American Waltham Watch Company* (1905).
Aked, Charles. *Horological Patents up to 1853* (1975).
Baillie, G. H. *Watchmakers and Clockmakers of the World* (1951 edn.)
Baillie, G. H., Clutton, C., and Ilbert, C., *Britten's Clocks and Watches* (1957).
Britten, F. J. *Watch and Clockmakers Handbook* (1st edn., 1884).
Britten, F. J. *Former Clock and Watch Makers and their Work* (1st edn., 1894).
Britten, F. J. *Old Clocks and Watches and their Makers* (6th edn., 1932).
Bruton, Eric. *Clocks and Watches 1400 to 1900* (1967).
Bruton, Eric. *Clocks and Watches* (1968).
Bruton, Eric. *Clock Collecting* (1974).
Bruton, Eric. *Clocks and Watches* (1974).
Buckley, Francis. *Old Manchester Clock and Watchmakers* (Privately published, Manchester Museum, 1925).
Buckley, Francis. *Old Watchmakers—Ellicott* (1930).
Camerer Cuss, T. P. *The Country Life Book of Watches* (1967), (New edn., 1977).
Camerer Cuss, T. P. *Early Watches* (1971).
Camm, F. J. *Watches; Adjustment and Repair* (5th edn., 1946).
Cescinsky, H., and Webster, M. R. *English Domestic Clocks* (1913; 1969 edn.).
Chamberlain, Paul M. *It's About Time* (1941).
Chapuis, Alfred, and Jacquet Eugene, *The Swiss Watch* (1953; 1970 reprint).
Clutton, Cecil, and Daniels, George. *Watches* (1965).
Cripps, W. J. *Old English Plate* (1967 edn.).
Cumhaill, P. W. *Investing in Clocks and Watches* (1967).
Daniels, George. *English and American Watches* (1967).
de Carle, Donald. *Practical Watch Repairing* (1969).
de Carle, Donald. *Watch and Clock Encyclopedia* (1975 edn.).
English Watches. Victoria and Albert Museum (1969).
Exhibition of British Clocks and Watches, Birmingham, 1954.
Fletcher, D. W. *Watch Repairing* (1964).
George Graham Bicentenary Exhibition, Catalogue of Exhibition, 1951.
Good, R. The First Lever Watch by Mudge. Reprint from *Horol. Journ.*, Dec. 1956.
Harris, H. G. *Watch and Clock Repairs* (1967).
Harwood, John. The Harwood Automatic, ext. *Jeweller and Met. Worker*, July 1960.
Hasluck, P. N. *The Clock Jobber's Handbook* (12th edn., 1948).
Hayward, J. F. *English Watches in the Victoria and Albert Museum* (1956).
Peate, I. C. *Clock and Watch Makers in Wales* (1960).
Pioneers of Precision Timekeeping, Monograph No. 3, Ant. Horol. Society.
Player, J. W. *Watch Repairing* (1945).

Smith, John. *Old Scottish Clockmakers* (*1453–1850*) (2nd edn., 1921).
Swinburne, J. *The Mechanism of the Watch* (1950).
Symonds, R. W. *A History of English Clocks*, (1947).
Torrens, D. S. Notes on Machine Watchmaking, *Horol. Journ.*, April 1947, p. 177.
Tremayne, Arthur. *Everybody's Watches* (c.1939).
Tyler, E. J. *European Clocks* (1968).
Tyler, E. J. *The Craft of the Watchmaker* (1973).
Ullyett, K. *Watch Collecting* (1970).
Ullyett, K. *Clocks and Watches* (1971).
White, Allen. *The Chain Makers* (1967).

Missing from the Library and as yet unobtainable:
Baillie, G. H. *Watches* (1929), (consulted).
Camerer Cuss, T. P. *The Story of Watches* (1952).

Index

Abbott, Henry G., 22
Accessories, watch, 107
Ainge, Alexander, 83
Aked, Charles, 61, 75
Alacrity movement, 47
Albert watch chain, 47, 109
Antiquarian Horology, 49, 128
Arnold, John, 36
Assay offices, 101, 115
A.W.W. Co. (*see* Waltham)

Baillie, G. H., 49, 57, 69, 76, 117
Baird, W. & J., 74
Balance cock, 81, 83
Balance spring, 55, 86, 88
Balance staff, 123
Barraud, P. P., 75
Barwise, John, 43, 79, 80
Bellion, William, 51
Benson and Co., 41, 51
Benson Bros., 34, 41, 90
Birch key, 108
Birmingham hallmark, 41, 50
Boer War, 36
Bosley, Joseph, 86
Bosley regulator, 60, 86
"Bovets", 20
Breguet, 21, 80
British Horological Institution, 126
British Watch Co., 17, 43, 79
Britten, F. J., 11, 49, 57, 72, 79, 82
Brownhill, John, 40
Bruton, Eric, 36, 49, 82, 120
Bullion, 50, 94
Bull's-eye flat, 66

Butterfield (Liverpool), 51

Camerer Cuss, T. P., 49, 86
Cases, 89
  Badge and garter, 99
  Bows, 114
  Britannia silver, 96
  Carat values, 93, 94
  Case duty, 96, 116
  Casemakers, 89
  Casemakers' initials, 96
  Case materials, 93
  Consular case, 49, 58
  Crystal, 130
  Demi-hunter case, 46, 58
  Dennison Watch Case Co., 90
  Double-bottomed case, 41
  Engine turned, 98
  Gilt, 95
  Hallmarks, 93, 96, 115
  Hinge shape, 59, 92
  Hunter case, 58, 103
  Illinois Watch Case Co., 29
  Keystone Case Co., 29
  Lancashire size range, 90
  Monogram, 99
  Pinchbeck, 95
  Recasing, 100
  Rolled gold, 96, 97
  Shagreen, 66, 67
  Sterling silver, 96
Centre-seconds chronograph, 45
"Chaffers'" hallmarks, 115
Chaffcutter verge, 77
Chainmaker's, The, 49
Chapman, Denis, 136

Chapuis, A., 16
Chamberlain, Paul M., 39, 53, 55, 73, 86
Chamois leather bags, 90, 110
Chester hallmark, 50
Chinese market, 20
Chisholm and Co., 84
Chronometer Escapement, 45, 80
Clerkenwell, 50, 59, 70
Clockmakers' Company, 117, 118
Clutton and Daniels, 21, 48, 61, 65, 76
Collecting, 127
Consular case, 49, 58
Cooper, Edward, 72
Cornwall, James, 81
Coventry, 41, 43, 47, 50, 60, 89
Crank lever escapement, 81
Cumhaill, P. W., 49, 71
Cylinder escapement, (*see* Escapement)

Daniels, George, 49
Debaufre, Peter, 77
De Carle, Donald, 11, 49
Deck watch, 60
Demi-hunter, 46, 58
Dennison, Aaron L., 23, 28, 90
Dennison Watch Case Co., 19, 24, 90
Detached lever (*see* Lever)
Dials
   Champlevé, 71, 72
   Metal, 66, 71
   Porcelain, 52, 66
   White, 52
Double-bottomed case, 41
"Draw", 54
Dress Watch, 104
Drinkwater (Coventry), 47
Dummy barrel, 40
Dust cover, 67

Earnshaw, Thomas, 48, 59, 79, 83
Ébauche, 17, 18, 119
Edward VII, 37
Elgin Watch Co., 22, 32
English lever, 39
Escapements, 113
   Chronometer, 45, 80
   Crank lever, 81
   Cylinder, 48, 54, 65, 74
   Detached lever, 48, 54
   Duplex, 54, 65, 78
   Ormskirk verge, 54, 77
   Rack lever, 54, 75

"Finissage", 17
Fobs, 108
Fob watches, 105
Forest (London), 51
Free sprung watch, 88
Frictional rest, 54
Fusee lever watch, 48
   Balance cocks, 52
   Decorated dials, 52
   Elegance, 52
   "Detached patent", 53
   Period, 50
   Regulation (*see* Bosley)

Going barrel, 39
Going fusee, 49, 84
Gold hinges, 46
"Gold rush", 101, 120
Goliath watch, 104
Grandfather's watch, 22
Graham, George, 74, 75
Graham, Jno., 75
Graves (Sheffield), 41
Great-grandfather's watch, 22
Green, Robert, 67, 69
Greenwich Mean Time, 62
"Grey" movements, 17, 43
Grimlade and Johnson, 79
Gronow, Captain, 80

Hairspring, 86, 88
Half-hunter case, 46, 58
Hallmarks, 93, 96, 115
Hallmark guide, 93
Hamilton Watch Co., 22, 32
Hands
   Arrowhead, 67
   Beetle-and-poker, 66, 72
   Breguet, 67
   Fleur-de-Lys, 52
   Jewelled, 67
   Pierced, 67
   Spade, 67
Handsworth, 90
Hargreaves, John, 47
Harrison, John, 49
Harwood, John, 38
Hewitt, T. P., 43
Hick, Matt, 58
Hook, 55
Hornby, James, 51, 81
Hornby, Richard, 51

Horological Journal, 128
Houghton, James, 78
Houghton, Thomas, 78
Hunter cases, 46, 58, 103

Ilbert Collection, 74, 76
Illinois Watch Case Co., 29
Ingersol watch, 27
Ingold, Frederick, 43
Interchangeability, 17

Jarvis, John, 60
Jewelling, 55
John Bull watch, 44

K. & D. Watch Tool Co., 108
Kellie, John, 47, 88
Kew, 18
Keyless work, 41
Keys, 107
Key set, 48
Key wind, 41

Ladies' fob watch, 105
Lancashire range, 90
Lancashire Watch Co., 15, 23, 42
Lapel strap/chain, 109
Lever escapement, (*see* Escapement)
Leverization, 82
Lignes, 90
Lister, William, 77
Litherland, Peter, 75
Litherland & Co. (etc.), 75, 76
Liverpool, 43, 50
Liverpool jewelling, 51, 77
Liverpool Museum, 44, 71, 81, 89
Local time, 62
London hallmark, 50, 51, 59
Loomes, Brian, 121
Lossier hairspring, 32
Lunate counterpoise, 74

Maintaining power, 49
Mason, Ezechial, 81
Mason, Hester, 51
Massacre of the Watches, 134
Massey, Edward, 81
Massey, F. J., 81
Medallions, 110
Mershon's patent, 31
Meyer (Manchester), 51

Mudge, Thomas, 48, 102, 112

Napoleon, 58, 80
Newsome (Coventry), 47

Oignons, 71
Olivettes, 40
Ormskirk verge, 79

Paircase, 52
Pearson, E. A., 36
Phillips, Robert, 15, 70, 83, 125, 135
Photography, 132
Pillar, balluster, 67
Pinchbeck, 95
Pin pallet, 16
Pocket sundial, 62
Polding, J. B., 39
Prescot, 35, 43, 54
"Preston haul", 18
Provenance, 112
Push piece, 40

Quare, Daniel, 72
Quartz crystal, 38
Queen Elizabeth's watch, 36

Rack lever, 54, 75
Railway time, 62
Railway watch, 34
Recasing, 100
Records, 131
Reed, George P., 31, 88
Regulation, 85
  Bosley, 60, 86
  Free sprung, 88
  Index, 88
  Mershon's patent, 31
  Micrometer, 88
  Modified Bosley, 88
  Tompion, 58, 85
  Tompion blank, 59, 86
  Tompion rosette, 58, 67, 72, 85
  Whiplash, 31
Repairs, 124
Restoration, 122
Robins, Royal E., 31
Roskell, Robt., 51, 77, 81
Roskopf, G. F., 16
Rotheram & Sons, 47, 84
Rough movement (*see* ébauche)
Rowley, Will, 53

Russells of Liverpool, 15, 41, 42
Rylands, James, 77
Rylands, Joshua, 77

Samuel (Manchester), 51
Savoury (London), 51
Security, 132
Seed, John, 78
Setting-up square, 59, 67
Sewill, Joseph, 47
Shagreen, 66, 67
Side setting, 40, 42
Sleeve setting, 42
Sliding button, 40, 42
Smith, Stanley, 15, 28, 88, 135
Smiths Watch Co., 26
Stopwatch, 46
Stopwork, 46
Sundail, 62
Sundial time, 62
Sweep hand, 45
Sweep seconds, 45
Swing ring, 30
Swiss Watches
  Development, 16
  Jacquet & Chapuis, 16
  Swiss movement makers, 19
  Swiss watch parts catalogue, 19

Tanner, Wm., 59
"The Field" (Benson), 18
Thelwell, Richard, 87
Three-quarter plate movement, 45, 88
Timing machine, 88
Tobias, Morris, 60
Tompion, Thomas, 55
Torrens, D. S., 16, 101, 136
Tortoiseshell, 66
Treherne, Alan, 81
Tyler, E. J., 40, 49

Value Added Tax, 14, 50, 95, 128
Vernon, Richard, 72
Verge Watch, 55
  Bows, 58, 66
  Case hinge, 58, 66
  Catgut lines, 55
  Chain, 55
  Consular case, 49, 58
  Eighteenth-century verge, 65, 71
  Farmer's Watch, 59
  Hairspring, 55
  Nineteenth-century verge, 57
  Pair cases, 58
  Pendant, 55, 66
  Regulation, 58, 59
  Sight glass, 58
  Sprung verge, 55, 71
  Tangent screw, 59, 67

Waltham watches
  Abbott, Henry G., 22
  American Waltham Watch Co., 22, 27
  Bartlett, P. S., movement, 31
  Crescent Garden movement, 26
  Fifteen-jewel movement, 30
  Full-plate movement, 27
  Going (motor) barrel, 27
  History of Waltham, 22
  Mass production, 24
  Movement numbers and table, 25
  Nine-jewel movement, 30
  Premier movement, 30
  River Charles, 31
  Riverside Maximus movement, 32, 33, 34
  Riverside movement, 30, 31
  Royal movement, 31
  Seven-jewel movement, 29
  Seventeen-jewel movement, 31
  Twenty-one jewel movement, 32
  Vanguard movement, 32
  Waltham (Mass.), 23
  Waltham Watch Cases, 24
  Waltham Watch Co., 22, 27
Waterbury watch, 27
Waterloo, 50
White, Allan, 49
Willatts, John, 75
Wise (Manchester), 51
Wristlet watch, 36

1. A modern Swiss pocket watch. A demi-hunter, cased in this country by A. L. Dennison, case hallmarked Birmingham 1938. The movement is stamped Swiss made under the trade name of Rolex. Of 15-jewel standard it is tested for temperature and rated in three positions. Regulation is by a simple index, and there is a compensation balance and clubfooted escape wheel teeth.

2. A Swiss movement, labelled as such, imported by and re-written for, a local retailer. The number of jewels is significantly not stated and it is probable that this is a 10-jewel movement. Cased in an A.L.D. case.

3. The elegant dial of an open-faced pocket watch signed William Bent of London, but carrying a Swiss movement. It was cased in Switzerland and imported complete. Inscribed for presentation in 1906. Keyless winding and sleeve hand setting.

4. The movement of watch above. It is a typical bar lever pattern much favoured by Swiss makers. It is of good quality with 17 jewels, but only a plain index. The clubfooted escape wheel teeth are clearly shown. There is no indication of the actual maker but it is fully signed by the London retailer.

5. Two characteristic Waltham watches of the early twentieth century, one of which has had the dial written for the retailer. Both are demi-hunters as shown by the double spade on the hour hand so that it can be more easily read through the lunette glass. The winding stem is opposite three o'clock as with all hunters and demi-hunters.

6. The Waltham 7-jewel Traveller watch. Note the unjewelled holes in the overall machine decoration of the chrome or nickelled back plate. The number is in the 27 million range, i.e., made about 1930.

7. The Waltham 15-jewel watch. The extra jewelling can be seen together with the more sophisticated star wheel regulator. The centre wheel pivot hole remained un-jewelled. The movement was fitted into an A.L.D. case and held in place by the dog screws. Serial number is 22 million, so manufactured about 1922.

8. The 17-jewel Waltham. Very similar to the 15-jewel movement with addition of jewelling to the centre wheel pivot. In an A.L.D. case and made about 1922.

9. The 17-jewel Royal movement. The better quality in comparison to the plain 17-jewel movement is indicated by the word adjusted. It is also noticeable that the jewelling of the centre, third and fourth wheels is set into a collet and held in place by screws. The movement would be manufactured about 1914 and is cased in an A.L.D. case.

10. The P. S. Bartlett 17-jewel movement. In appearance very little different from the Royal movement. Manufactured in the early 1920's and cased in an A.L.D. case.

11. The 19-jewel Riverside movement. A very high-class watch, the greater care in its production being indicated by the information that it has been adjusted in five positions. The number of 15 million suggests manufacture about 1910.

12. The 23-jewel Vanguard credited with a Lossier terminal curve hair spring and six positions. It also has on the dial a subsidiary up and down dial to indicate the extent to which the mainspring is wound up. The finish is relatively poor for such a very fully jewelled watch.

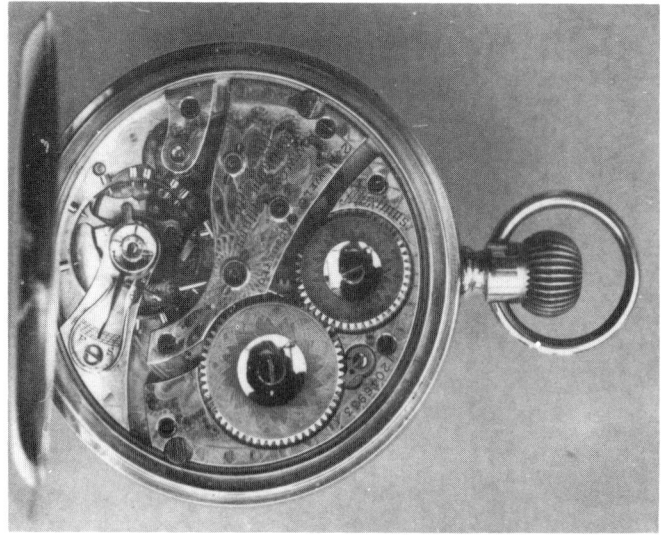

13. The 23-jewel Riverside Maximus — the ultimate in Waltham movements. It is basically named a Riverside with the Maximus discretely tucked away. The regulator is of the whiplash pattern. With a number in the 12 million band it was probably made about 1905. It has wheels of a low-carat gold composition.

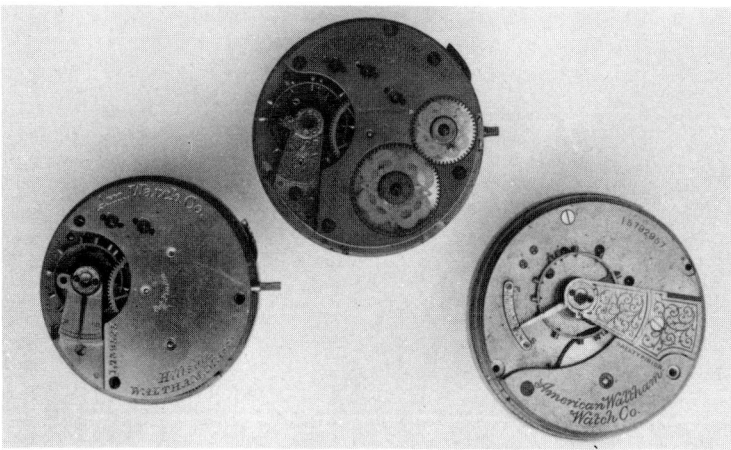

14. Some older Waltham movements.
Left: the Hillside three-quarter plate, apparently 13-jewels. Numbered 1.7 million and named Am. Watch Coy. it was made before 1885.
Centre: a three-quarter plate, good quality 15-jewel movement with a 3 million number, probably dated about 1888. It is labelled A.W.W. Co. and named as a Riverside.
Right: a full plate pattern of about 1909.

15. Further Waltham movements.
Left: a full plate 15-jewel movement of about 1914. Screw regulator.
Centre: another Riverside movement, but only 15 jewels. Note the regulator — an eccentric cam type.
Right: a 7-jewel movement with the name of Ensign.

16. Key wound Elgin watch in a bulky silver case. Cased in America, therefore no hallmark to date the watch. Probably about 1890. Note hair line dial cracks.

17. Top plate of movement of Elgin watch. Full plate with old fashioned cock and simple steel balance. Bosley type regulation. Minimal jewelling and signed Elgin Natl. Watch Co. Key wound and key hand set.

18. Elgin 21-jewel movement. Cased in a lightweight 18 K. case by Keystone Case Co. No hallmark to date the watch. Note the bar bridges for the third, fourth and escape wheels and the very sophisticated screw adjustment. The quality of this movement is about on par with the Waltham Riverside Maximus. In 1960 this watch was sold to me at a fair market value of £17.10.0 when gold was at a low and controlled price.

19. The Hamilton 17-jewel movement. A rather plain movement cased in a 9-carat A.L.D. case, hallmarked 1939. Note the whiplash regulator. This was missing when the watch was bought but Hamilton supplied and fitted a new one. The only two other Hamiltons in my collection are both 21-jewel movements.

20. The classic English lever of about 1890. In a heavy silver case with a push piece on the stem to open the back. This is a keywind fusee with hand setting by a square on the main arbor.

21. The back of the watch shown in Illustration No. 20. The double bottom case has a background of engine-turning and a milled edge. The badge and garter motif is almost universal. The bow is pinned with a screw and the movement hinges forward. Case maker's initials on the stem.

22. An English lever from the Lancashire Watch Co. of Prescot — rather dubiously referred to in my index as an example of the Prescot turnip. Case hallmarked Chester 1902, in heavy silver with gold hinge pins. Hands fleur-de-lis. The whole styling shows the clinging to the old Prescot tradition and carrying it into the twentieth century.

23. A pair of watches reputed to have been owned by brothers. Note the close serial numbers, one watch being case-dated Birmingham 1898, and the other Birmingham 1899. Both are key wound and have dummy barrels. The hinge on which the movement swung forward can be seen together with the push piece in the stem for opening the back.

24. 15-jewelled English lever by Benson in a handsome engine-turned full hunter case. Case-dated London 1920 which is out of keeping with the side hand set with olivettes. The watch has seen very little wear as shown by the unworn bow, the engine-turning and the unmarked screw heads.

25. English lever by Penlington and Batty of Liverpool. Note the side setting with olivettes and wear on the bow. The case had three dents which needed the attention of the case repairer. The movement is an English three-quarter plate with 15 jewels. Case-dated London 1890.

26. Three-quarter plate lever by Henry Nalson of London, case-dated London 1897. The case, a demi-hunter shows minimum wear as if a "Sunday watch". Close inspection shows the spur toothed English type of escape wheel. Fifteen jewels are set in with collets. The prominent collet with three holding screws is a vestigial remnant of the key winding days.

27. A modest open faced English lever by R. C. Oldfield of Liverpool. The silver case is hallmarked Birmingham 1892, suggesting a Coventry origin.

28. An unusually large and very heavy piece finished to a very high standard. It is far too heavy to be carried in the pocket and the bow shows no sign of wear from a watch chain. Perhaps it is a deck watch. The spur toothed English type escape wheel is clearly seen. It is case-dated London 1897.

29. A flyback chronograph. The first pressure on the side button brings the sweep hand to zero, the second starts it off and the third brings it back again. Hand setting is by the slide out release at five o'clock. The case is engraved for presentation in 1890. The movement is Swiss — possibly by Longines. As shown by the stem being at three o'clock this is a hunter case.

30. Fusee lever by John Chesworth of Prescot, case-dated Chester 1845. Ironically though millions of movements in the rough were made at Prescot, this is my only example of a watch finished and retailed by an individual watchmaker of the township.

31. A fine demi-hunter cased centre seconds chronograph by John Kellie of Liverpool. Case hallmarked Chester 1893. Keyless winding and side setting.

32. The rather beautifully written top plate of the John Kellie watch. Note the "dog screws", half cut away, holding the movement in the case.

33. The well-written dial of the watch by John Kellie. Sunk centre with short hour hand without a second spade. Outer chapter in seconds with divisions to fifth seconds. Gold hands and black counterbalanced seconds sweep. Another similar full hunter watch by same maker (hallmarked Chester 1900) is "free sprung", i.e., has no regulator.

34. Another fine chronograph by J. Hargreaves of Liverpool. In a full hunter case, hallmarked Chester 1900. Keyless, but note the old-fashioned screw fitting of the bow. The hands are original and in gold. The sweep hand is attractively counterbalanced by a ring rather than the more usual spade.

35. The top plate of the watch by Hargreaves showing dog screws. The small spur toothed escape wheel can just be made out. The side setting push piece is rather crudely guarded by a V-cut projection rather than more gently sloping and later olivettes.

36. A good-quality centre seconds watch by Pearce of Leeds. It is difficult to know whether this should be called a chronograph since it has no stop-work and no outside slide button. Case-dated London 1902.

37. A high-quality chronograph by W. Samuel of Manchester. Case in 18-carat gold and hallmarked Chester 1905. Three-quarter plate with machined design. Spur toothed escape wheel of the English pattern, probably made in Coventry or Prescot.

38. Characteristic example of a later fusee lever, case-dated Birmingham 1890. The silver case has edge milling, and garter and badge motif on back. The movement, which is unnamed, swings out on the hinge at twelve o'clock. The balance is modern bimetallic with timing screws. The dust cover has the usual sliding clip. It is key wound and the hand setting is by square on the centre arbor.

39. A late fusee lever signed Meyer of Manchester, with case hallmarked Chester 1898. The full top plate is pinned in position with an engraved cock and Bosley regulation. The balance is bimetallic with timing screws. Key wind. There is minimal jewelling. The case is single bottom with dust cover, suggestive of the conservative Prescot manufacture.

40. A late fusee lever by T. R. Russell of Liverpool, case-dated Chester 1890. Full plate, minimal jewelling and modern bimetallic balance. Almost certainly a Prescot movement.

Below, left.
41. An early fusee lever by William Rowley of Liverpool. The case has a double hallmarking, Chester 1836 and London 1833. The top plate is pinned, and the jewelling minimal. The balance is plain and in gold. The regulation is of the Bosley type. On the cock are the words "Patent" and "Detatched".

Below, right.
42. The graceful dial of the William Rowley watch. Breguet hands in gold. Tall slender numerals. The seconds dial is of the large size usual for this period. In a single Consular case.

43. An early fusee lever of unusual design by Richard Thelwell of Manchester, case-dated Chester 1834. Instead of a full dust cover there is a flat hinged rim fitting round the edge of the movement. The spur toothed English type of escape wheel is seen. A modern index is fitted to the cock instead of the more usual Bosley pattern, but the balance wheel remains simple. Thelwell's address is given as 3, St. Anne's Square, Manchester, with a date (by Britten) of 1836.

44. Early fusee lever dial with tall numerals. The hands are original — gold fleur-de-lys. The seconds dial is large.

45. Fusee lever by Savoury and Son, Cornhill, London — case-dated London 1841. The case is engine-turned and decorated. There is a gold decorated dial with gold numerals. The hands, in black heavy double swell spade pattern, are original but not easy to read against the background. The square for hand setting and the top movement hinge are clear.

46. A beautifully cased fusee lever by Hester Mason of Liverpool — case-dated Chester 1869. There is another watch of the same date by the same maker in the Liverpool museum. The case is decorated and engine-turned. The dial is gold with gold numerals while the spade hands are also in gold.

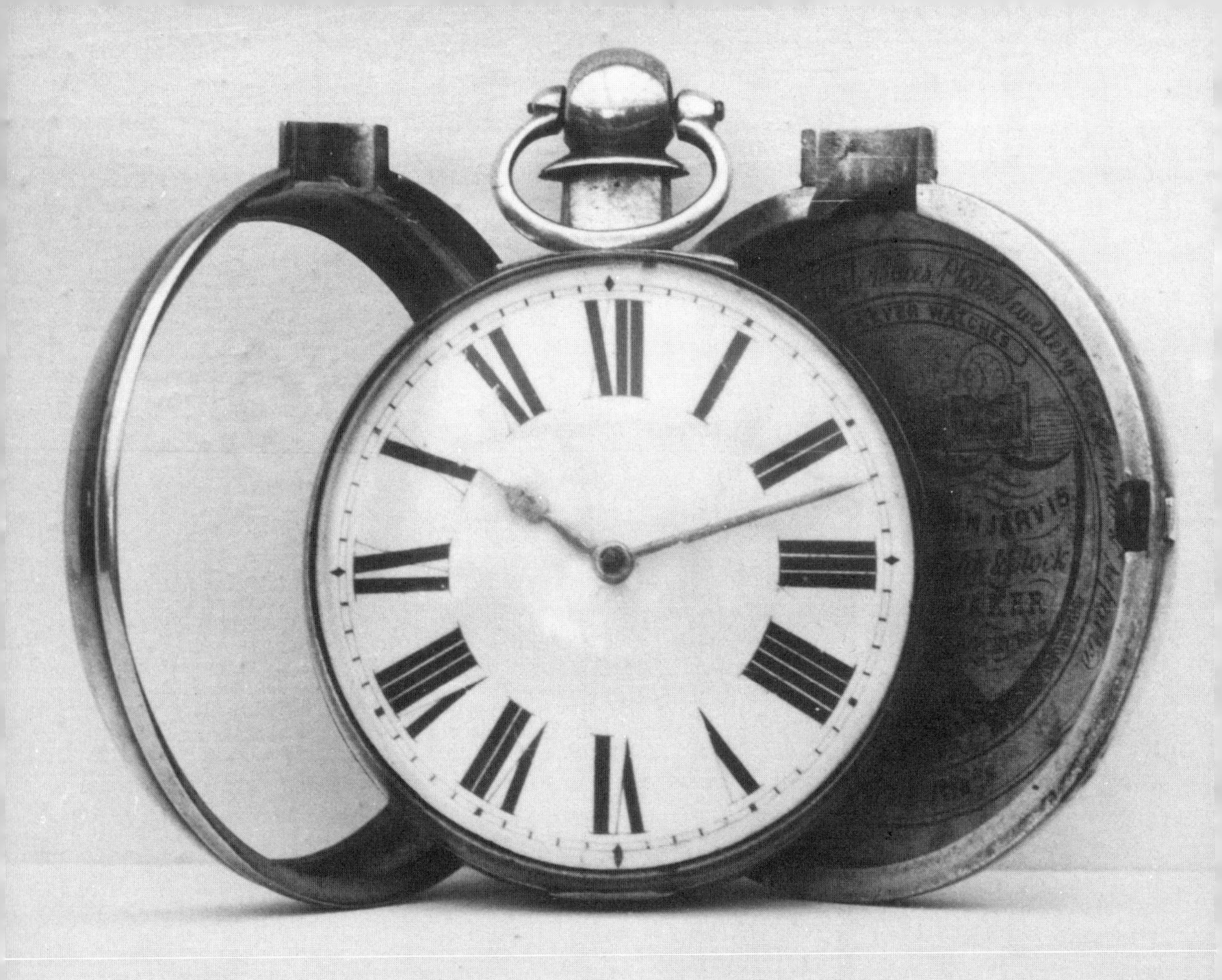

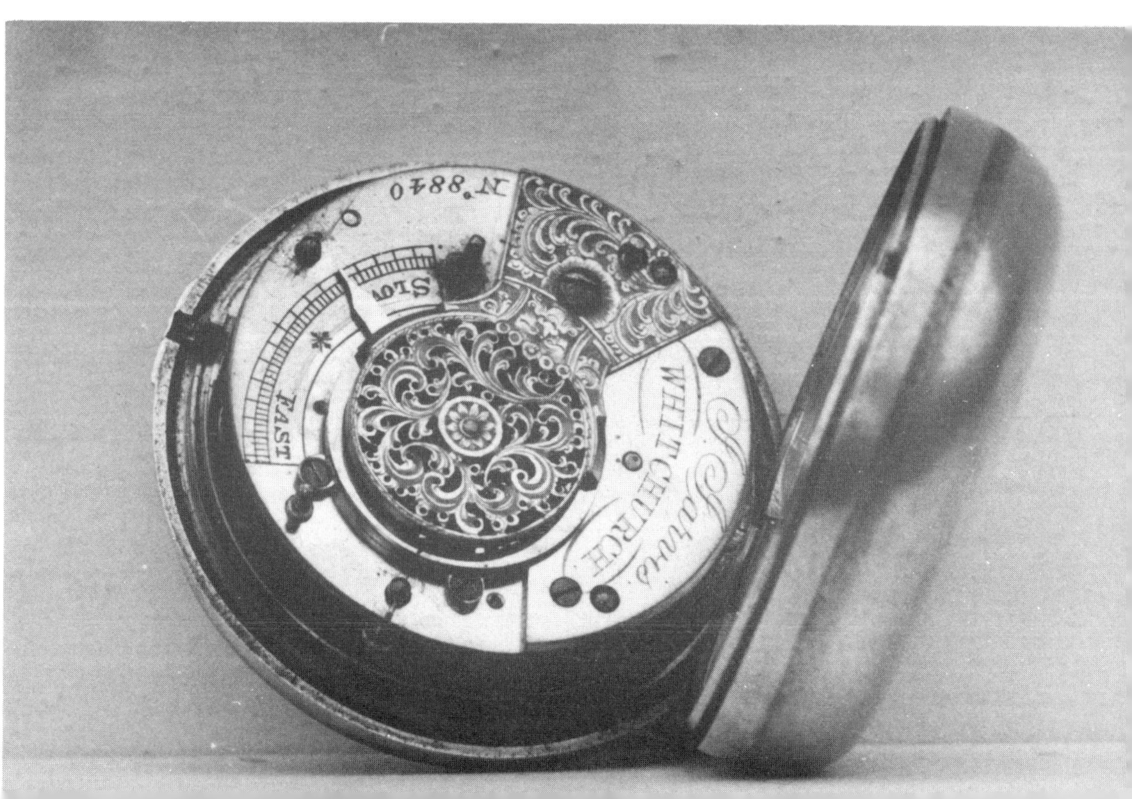
N° 8840
Slow
FAST
WHITCHURCH

49. A mid-nineteenth-century verge with painted dial, case-dated London 1850. The artist's signature may be seen at the bottom of the picture — many other types of scene were in common use. The movement is engraved Wm. Tanner of Lewes.

Opposite:

47. Typical mid-nineteenth-century verge named for J. Jarvis of Whitchurch. The case, hallmarked Birmingham 1847, is heavy to the point of being a turnip. The outer case carries the watch paper with repair dates on the back. The stem is wide oval in section and the bow held with a screw pin. It is probable that the whole piece was made in Coventry or Birmingham and engraved for the retailer. It is reported to have been in the same family since it was originally purchased.

48. The movement of the Jarvis watch, showing the earlier type of decorated and pierced cock. The Bosley regulator is also of the earlier period.

50. A half-hunter single cased verge by Thos. Mawkes of Derby, case-dated Birmingham 1814. The use of letters instead of numerals in the outer chapter — S. James, Chester — perhaps refers to the first owner. The inner chapter ring can be read through the lunette glass. There is dial winding and the dial itself is poor and cracked.

51. The movement of the watch by Mawkes of Derby giving, incidentally, a better view of the single case arrangement. Unlike later half-hunters the movement is hinged at nine o'clock, and the movement has not been rotated so that three o'clock is in the stem position. Regulation is of the Bosley pattern under a decorated and pierced cock. The older arrangement by Tompion is still present. The square on the arbor remains but the dial is blanked out by a blued steel collet.

52. Dial of demi-hunter verge in a single Consular case, case-dated London 1820. Hunter cases were relatively rare in eighteenth-century verges, in comparison with double open-faced watches.

53. A neat and well-kept demi-hunter verge in a single Consular case. Maker, J. Newton, London (1815-24), case-dated London 1820. There is dial winding. This must be an early demi-hunter before the introduction of the double spade hour hand. It is not usual to have arabic numerals at this date.

54. A solid, no-nonsense nineteenth-century verge by a well-known provincial maker — Matthew Hick of York (1812-34). Case-dated London 1823. It remains in very good working order though the top plate shows much wear. Regulation is by the Bosley mechanism.

55. Nineteenth-century verge movements.
Left:
The older Tompion-type regulating dial blanked out by the blue steel collet and the movement made up with a Bosley type regulator.
Right:
By Robt. Jones of Ruthin, a well-known maker. The cock seems crude or unfinished.

A good quality nineteenth-century verge by Richard Ward of London, case-dated London 1817.
56. The dial with original but rather unusual hands.

57. The dust cover, inscribed, with cut out showing Tompion's rosette for regulation.

58. The movement, very fully written as was common in the high class movement. Note the hand pointing to the rosette for exact regulation.

59. Outward appearance of typical eighteenth-century verge. Some points to notice are: small deep shape; outer case hinge stands proud with champhered corners — earlier corners were square; push piece for opening outer case at three o'clock; bow usually of a flat D shape.

60. Similar to Illustration No. 59. The rather small and worn bow is supported by a (modern) chamois leather watch bag or pocket. The pierced and decorated hands show a French influence. The outer chapter of Arabic lettering is usual. By John Hilton of London — case hallmarked London 1786.

61. A very unusual dial to an eighteenth-century verge signed by Robert Innes of London, with case hallmarked London 1750. The numerals in Arabic lettering without minute numbering suggest replacement by a very much later dial. The filigree hands which have been repaired could be original. The rest of the watch appears authentic, and the outer case is shagreen covered.

62. Eighteenth-century verge showing the common "beetle and poker" hands. Again Arabic numerals in a single chapter.

63. The transition from eighteenth- to nineteenth-century verge style. Single cased with dial wind. The bow is flat and there is no seconds dial. Hands original in gold — spade double swell. By Grayhurst, London (1802). The case is in worn gilt and not hallmarked.

64. Classical double cased eighteenth-century verge by Bartholomew Davis of Preston in silver case dated London 1763. Despite its age, the case and movement are in good condition and it has been restored to working order. The hands are original, gold, and arrowhead style.

65. Inner case and movement of Illustration No. 64 showing in particular the depth in relation to the small diameter. A decorated columnar pillar is shown.

66. Two characteristic inner cases and dials of mid-eighteenth-century verges. Both have flat D bows and outer Arabic minute chapters.

67. Three examples of movements from the first half of the eighteenth-century. The dials are enamel or porcelain. The "beetle and poker" hands in black steel give a rather heavy and drab effect.

68. Dust covers are not a common feature in the eighteenth-century verge, but the maker usually took the opportunity of engraving his name on the raised portion covering the cock.

69. A fine verge by Archibald Coats of Wigan, (died 1797) — case-dated Chester 1788. An unusual feature is that the maker's name is engraved on a superimposed silver plate instead of on the top plate itself. The piece is in very good condition and all-original. Very similar movements from the Coats (or Coates) family are in the Wigan, Preston and Liverpool museums. All show the silver overlay.

70. An obviously recased movement by Ric: Gibbs of London (*ante* 1745). There is no jewelling as can be seen by the top pivot of the balance staff. Note the streamers or wings from the balance cock. Tompion's pattern of regulator.

71. An eighteenth-century verge signed by Thos. Worswick of Lancaster in a silver case of the usual proportions and hallmarked Chester 1774. The movement is unjewelled. Thomas Worswick (1752-1801) was a maker of repute and a freeman of Lancaster. There are three of his watches the Lancaster museum.

72. A mid-eighteenth-century verge by Rt. Barker of Liverpool, undated because in a gilt case. Again no jewelling and Tompion style regulation. Note the mythical liver bird at the base of the cock. There is a similar watch by the same maker in the Liverpool museum also undated. No dates have been traced .or this maker.

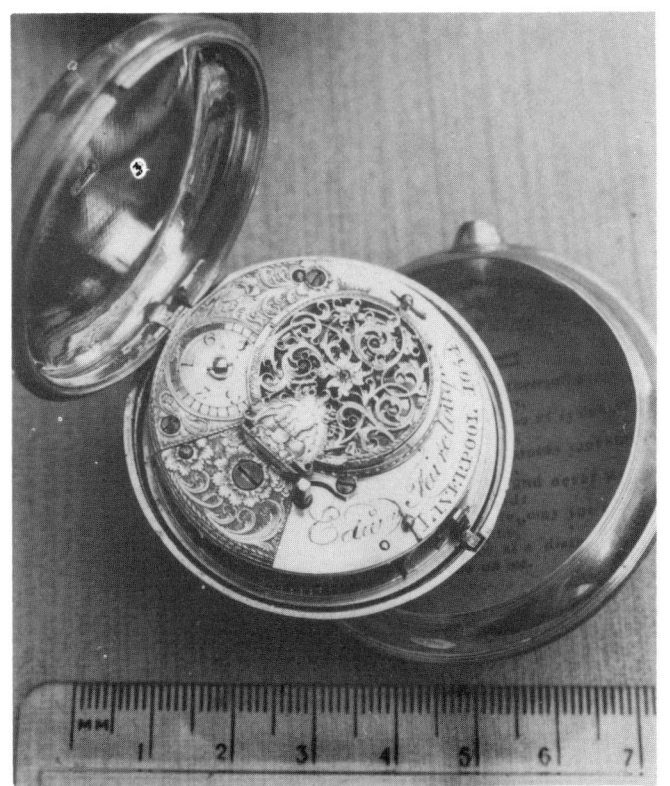

73. An eighteenth-century verge by Edw. Fairclough of Liverpool (1774-1803). The case is pinchbeck and not hallmarked, but the date 1788 is scratched inside the bezel. In the Liverpool museum there is a verge hallmarked Chester 1816. Loomes records Edw. Fairclough as having been a watchmaker in Castle Street from 1774 to 1800.

74. A verge by Geo. Booth of Manchester (1758, d. 1788) in a worn gilt case with no hallmark. A finely engraved cock, and beetle and poker hands. Regulation of the Bosley type with the Tompion rosette blanked off.

75. French eighteenth-century verge signed by Baillon of Paris. A François Baillon is listed by Baillie at Choudens in the second half of the eighteenth century. Two chapter rings. Dial and hands ornamented with paste.

76. Top plate of the watch illustrated above. Note the balance bridge instead of the English type cock — also coqueret. In all, the style and proportion is very similar to the English verge of the same era.

77. This most unusual elaborate skeleton verge is probably by Joseph Finney of Liverpool (b. 1703, d. 1772). The signature has been obliterated. Case-dated Chester 1804. The piece here is in the collection of a friend who asked me to photograph it, and it is reproduced with his permission. An almost similar piece, in this case a clubfoot verge, is to be seen in the Liverpool museum (hallmarked London 1771). This latter is illustrated on the cover of *Antiquarian Horology* Vol. 10, No. 1.

78. A very characteristic early eighteenth-century verge showing the large size and almost globular shape with a high domed glass. There may originally have been an outer case. There is no hallmarking as was not unusual at this time. This is by Edn. (?Edw.) Cooper of London, and the probable date is 1730-1740. A similar watch by the same maker is noted both by Baillie and Britten as being in the Dennison Collection. The watch has been restored by Mr. Gent of St. Helens, and is now in full working order.

79. The dial of the Cooper watch which is in silver with raised numerals and dial winding. The cast hands are beetle and poker. The bezel catch is of an early type.

80. Top plate of the Cooper verge. The cock shows lack of jewelling, it springs from well marked shelf and shows streamers at the base. Tompion pattern regulation. The decoration is pierced and screwed to the top plate. There is no movement number. Case maker's initials: S. I.

81. Side view of the Cooper movement showing its robust construction in thickness of cock, top plate and decoration. The balance is flat steel. Baluster pillars. The crown and contrate wheels are well shown.

82. A rather modern-looking cylinder escapement by George Wilson of London (1820). The single case is hallmarked London 1817. The top plate is plain and the balance wheel in simple steel. The cock is plain with regulation by a modern index. Apart from the fact that the hands are not original, the piece is, after being overhauled, in excellent condition.

83. A cylinder movement watch signed by Wm. Seymour of London (1766-1825), case hallmarked London 1785. The balance staff is jewelled on the ends and the balance is in flat steel. The cylinder is also in steel. A good quality piece restored to working order.

84. Cylinder movement by W. and T. Baird of London, showing the engraved dust cap. The firm was at 4 Hatton Garden from 1810 to 1830, but the case hallmark is later — London 1837. As befits a nineteenth-century movement the cock does not cover the balance which still remains of flat steel and is jewelled on the ends. Regulation is still by the Tompion method. Though there is naturally some wear on the steel cylinder the piece has been restored to working order.

85. An undistinguished French or Swiss cylinder movement.

86. Dial of a rack lever watch by Litherland and Co. of Liverpool, No. 2234, case-dated Chester 1802. The remarkable feature is that the seconds dial is only written for fifteen seconds and the seconds hand revolves four times every minute. The watch is in very good condition and keeps good time. An exactly similar watch, No. 2228 and hallmarked 1801, is shown in *Watches* by T. P. Camerer Cuss.

87. Top plate of Litherland watch. Patent written on the solid foot of the table-type cock. Regulator of the Bosley type. Rack lever escapement. No fourth wheel. Simple flat steel balance wheel with two arms.

88. Three Litherland movements:
Left:
By Litherland and Co. (No. 3630) is a rack lever very similar to Illustration No. 87.
Centre:
Another rack lever by Litherland, Whiteside and Co. (No. 6692).
Right:
A fusee lever by Litherland, Davies and Co. (No. 18177). Note the Liverpool jewelling.

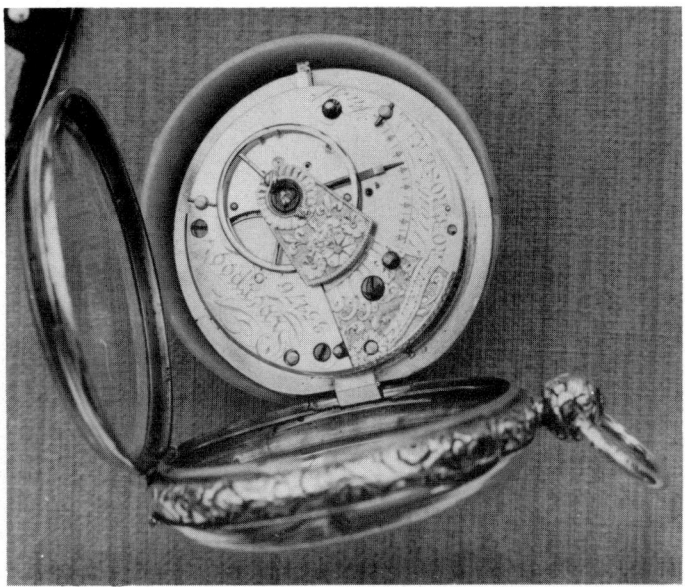

89. A rack lever by Robt. Roskell of Liverpool (No. 35476). In a single decorated case hallmarked London 1837. Roskell made many such movements.

90. A rack lever by (William) Lister of Newcastle-on-Tyne (1815-20) case-dated Chester 1815. The case is single, the whole piece is in good condition and the movement functions perfectly. Note Patent on foot of cock, jewelling on ends, and Bosley-type regulator.

91. Movements of the Ormskirk or clubfoot type: *Left:* Signed by John Seed of Wavertree (Liverpool). The name Edwd. Woods is engraved on the foot of the cock — possibly the first owner. *Right:* Signed by Josh. Ryland (late eighteenth-century) of Ormskirk.
These are very plain movements with decoration reduced to a minimum, unjewelled with flat steel balances.

92. A clubfoot verge signed by Jas. Houghton of Ormskirk (No. 461), James Houghton's dates are a little confused but he was previously assistant to Hugh Garrett of Ormskirk, also a maker of clubfoot verges. This movement is very plain and not in good condition. In the Liverpool museum there are two further clubfoot verge watches by James Houghton, Nos. 43 and 744.

93. Duplex movement by Thos. Earnshaw, London No. 3360. It is in a pair silver case hallmarked 1779. The rather fine dial and hands are original and undamaged.

94. Top plate of the Earnshaw duplex. The outstanding feature of this very fine movement is the cut (? bimetallic) balance with heavy weights. As there is no regulating index the movement would appear to be free sprung.

95. The well laid-out dial of a duplex watch (No. 525) by Grimalde and Johnson of London (1815-1825). Large seconds dial with the hand designed without counterpoise. Well-cut fleur-de-lys hands. Double silver case hallmarked rather inconsistently Birmingham 1834.

96. Top plate of the duplex watch by Grimalde and Johnson. Simple nineteenth-century type of cock with diamond endstones. Flat brass balance with Bosley-type regulation. Restored to full working order.

97. *Centre:* A rather fine verge movement by Thos. Earnshaw (No. 3813) which has been converted to a lever escapement. The movement has a dust cap which does not cover the cock and is cut out for the rosette. There is a diamond endstone. The balance wheel is plain steel. Winding is through the dial, though there is also a winding square through the top plate.
Left and right: Two similar eighteenth-century verge movements of a similar date.

98. Massey lever escapement by Jas. Cornwall of Liverpool (No. 782). It is difficult to make out the details of the escapement merely by looking between the plates and the balance cock needs to be removed.

99. Lever escapement by F. J. Massey (grandson of Edw. Massey) of Clerkenwell (No. 6088). In the photograph the lower segment dust cover has been removed and the escapement can be viewed directly.

100. Typical demi-hunter case from the 1920s housing a keyless Waltham movement. A chapter ring is engraved on the case outside the central lunette. The hour hand has a double spade and the hands are in gold.

101. Engine-turning on the back of a good quality English-made case. The keyless wind and the side hand setting with olivettes date it at the beginning of this century. There is very little wear.

102. Tortoiseshell-covered outer case of an eighteenth-century verge watch. Movement by Alex. Ainge, c. 1776. Period is indicated by the flat D bow and the external hinge with champhered corners.

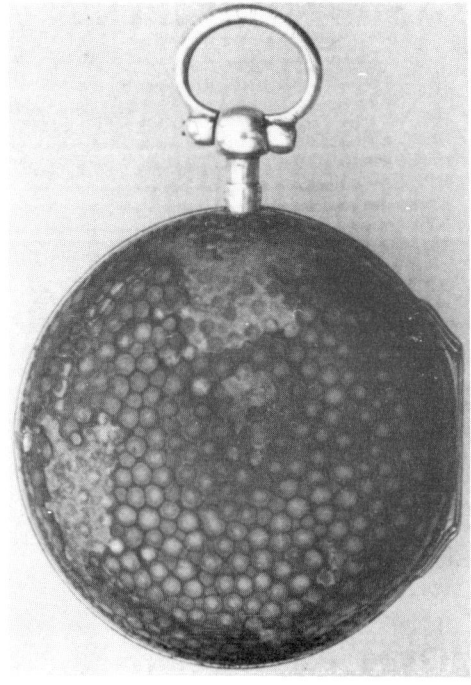

103. Shagreen-covered outer case of an eighteenth-century verge watch by Robt. Green of Liverpool, c. 1767. The covering is well-worn and bald in places.

104. Typical marks in the back of the watch case: *Top:* the Lion Passant indicating silver; *Left:* the anchor for the Birmingham Mint; *Right:* the date letter, in this case 1928; *Bottom:* the maker's initials — A.L.D. (A. L. Dennison) and his serial number. Jewellers' repair marks can also be seen.

105. Markings inside a rolled gold case. This is an A.L.D. Moon case, guaranteed to wear for twenty years without wearing through. Most significant is the absence of any hallmark.

106. The rolled gold guarantee and advertisement inside the dome of a case. The fact that the basis of the case metal is composition with a layer of gold on each side is made clear, but the mention of 10-carat gold misleads people to think of it as a gold case.

107. A common finding on gold watch cases — the large monogram of the original owner.

108. The inscribed presentation gold watch for long service.

109. The watch paper in the back of the watch illustrated as Nos. 47 and 48. This was the original advertisement of the man who signed the watch. It had been returned to the seller on several occasions and these dates together with name and address of the owner were written on the back of the paper.

110. This watch "paper" is in fact a sentimental verse printed on silk for retention as a memento. Packing such as this was often necessary to prevent the inner case rattling about inside the outer case as a result of wear. The watch in question is an eighteenth-century verge by Edward Fairclough of Liverpool.

111. A watchmaker's advertisement showing a rather gloomy philosophical verse.

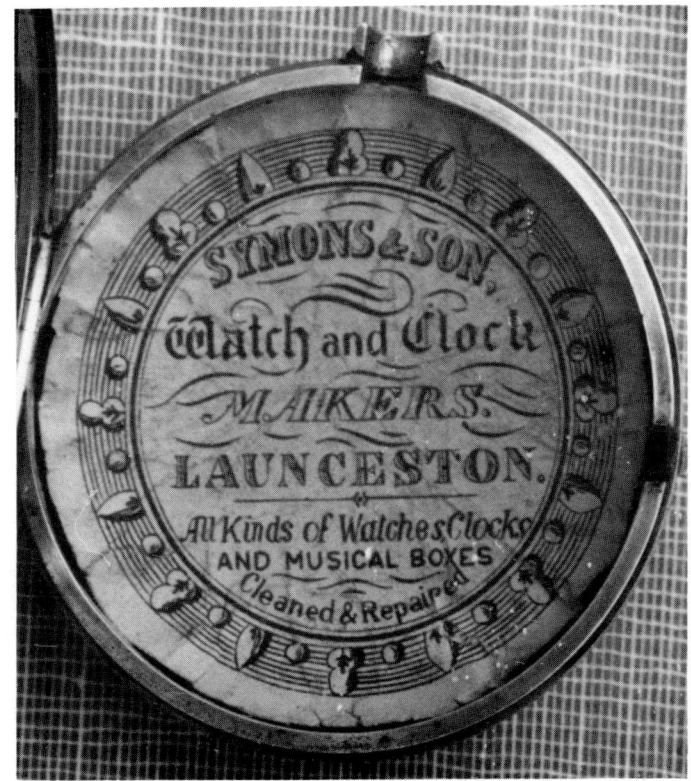

112. A watch paper showing the more standard advertisement.

113. A standard watch paper neatly cut round the edges to fit into the round of the outer case. Brian Loomes lists Wm. Simcock as being at 115-117 Bridge Street, Warrington, from 1848 to 1858.

115. A memento embroidered on a piece of silk for a young man to carry in his watch case.

114. A sentimental piece of embroidery overlaying the watch paper, enjoining the owner, whenever he consulted his watch to "Remember Me". Sometimes the lady's hair was used rather than silk.

116. An example of an exaggerated degree of Liverpool Jewelling in a movement by Richard Pickford of Liverpool, 1848-51. As usual the jewelling is in quartz.

117. Liverpool Jewelling by William Bellion of Liverpool *c.* 1877. In some instances the jewelling is confined to one or two "windows" but here it includes the winding arbour.

118. Liverpool Jewelling in a movement by James Hornby (1824-48). It is a top-grade movement as suggested among other things by the inclusion of the maker's address.

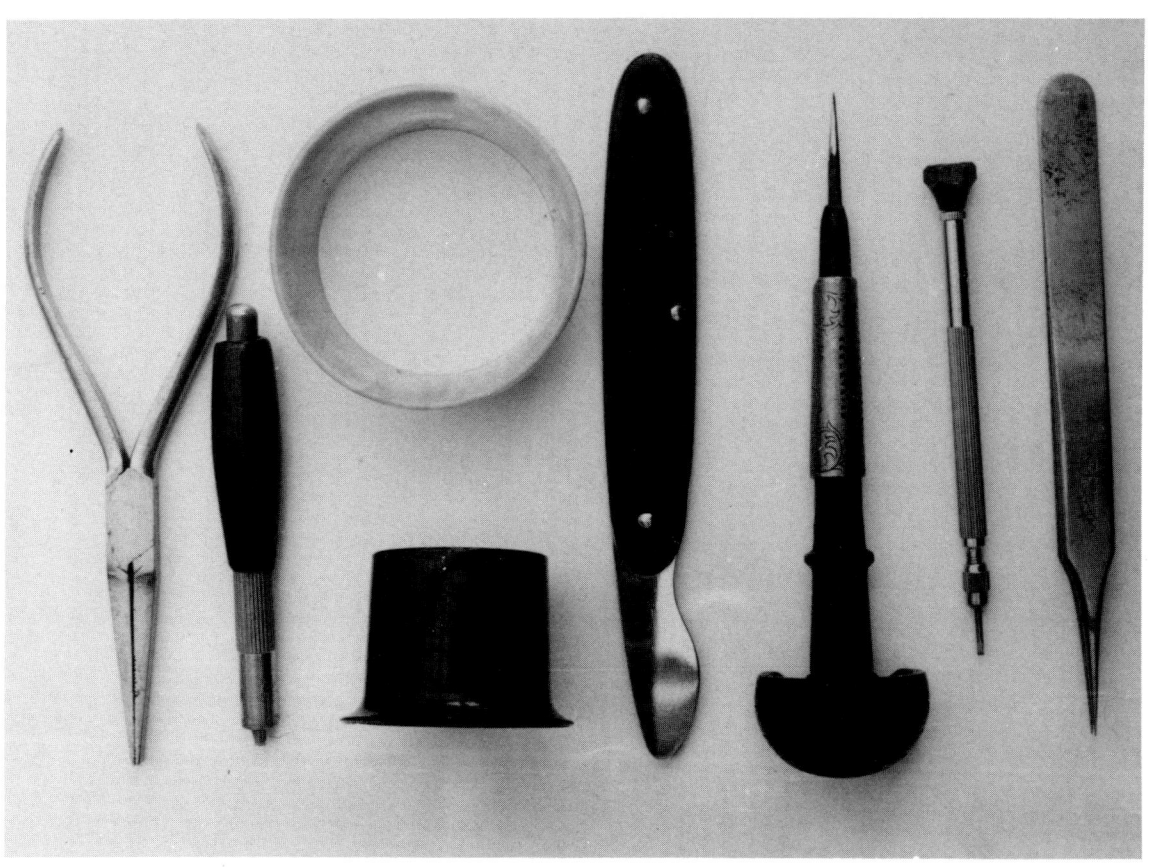

119. Some tools for the watch collector. Reading from left to right: pliers; Birch patent universal key; movement holder; eye glass; jeweller's watch-opening knife; pusher for hinge pins; watchmaker's screwdriver; tweezers.

120. Examples of commonplace watch keys for key wind movements of the last century. Two are universal keys. The rest are generally marked with their size, 1 to 12. Usually attached to the free end of the watch chain and carried in the waistcoat pocket where they become blocked by fluff.

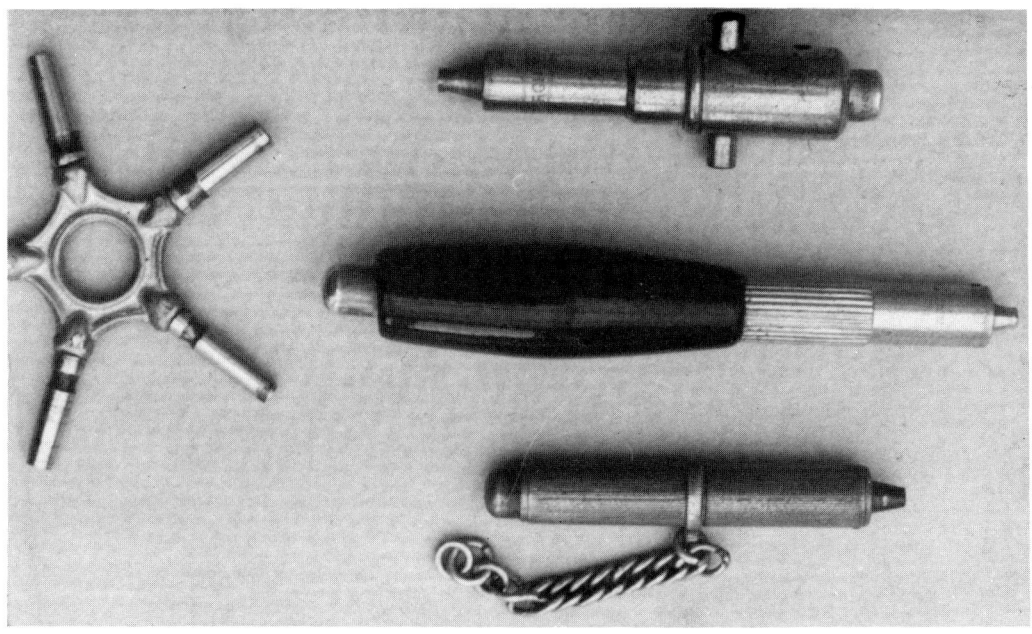

121. Three examples of the Birch universal key. These are all stamped Birch's patent. The centre example is that most commonly in use by watchmakers today. On the left is the star-shaped five or six-legged key.

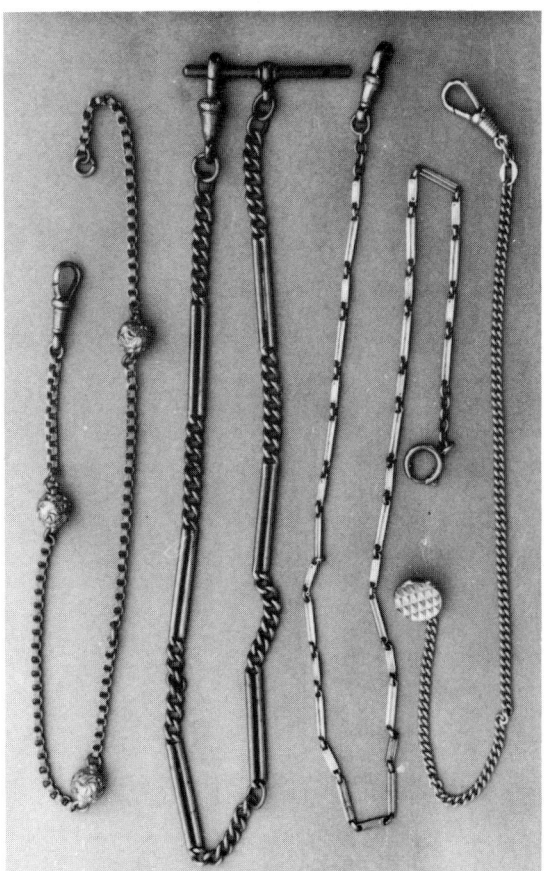

122. Two examples of the watch fob. Usually they are of black ribbed moire ribbon with fittings of gold. A seal or jewel is often found attached as in the example on the right.

123. Some examples of dress watch chains, mostly gilt. At the top is the modern curb anchored in the lapel button hole with the watch in the breast pocket.

124. The leather watch guard: *top:* strap and buckle to fasten through waistcoat or lapel button hole; *centre:* plaited leather strap; *bottom:* plain strap anchored through waistcoat button hole.

125. *Above left:* The classic double Albert chain in the popular curb link.

126. *Above right:* A single Albert chain in a variant of the link-and-fetter pattern. A sporting prize medallion hangs from the waistcoat button hole.

127. *Left:* A massive single Albert in chain link and tapering towards each end. This is in silver, hallmarked on every link and showing much wear.

128. Examples of prize sporting medallions worn on watchchains, giving indications of the wearers' sporting interests and prowess.

129. Fusee lever watch with single curb link Albert and medallion.

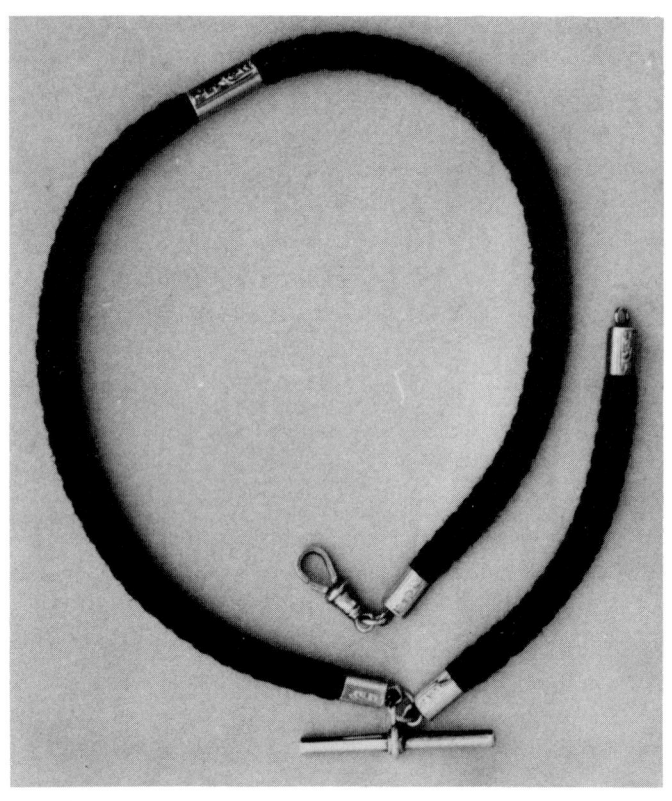

130. Victorian watch guard of woven horsehair — possibly a sign of mourning.

131. A simple boxwood bedside watch-stand with a transfer picture of Ryde. The watch is signed Trans Pacific and the movement is 21-jewel Swiss.

132. Movement of a fairly common type of Swiss Automaton. The figures appear to strike the hour. The case has long since been scrapped for its bullion value and the movement has been mounted for display purposes in a Perspex block.

133. Dress watches. Decorated hands, dials and cases were usual. *Left:* a simple Elgin 7-jewel movement with a worn dial but decorative bow, hands and an engine-turned case; *Right:* an Omega 17-jewel Swiss movement. The dial is decorated and the hands luminous tipped with raised gold letters. The case is an American Keystone.

134. An attractive silver engine-turned travelling watch-case with a monogram. There is a flap at the back for standing on the bedside table. The hallmark is London 1917.

135. A Goliath travelling watch-clock in a silver case. Case maker's initials S.B. and S.L., hallmarked Birmingham 1903. The watch is 2½ inches in diameter. It is a Swiss 30-hour bar lever movement with the club-footed escape wheel. It is in full repair.

136. Another example of the Goliath travelling watch. The decorated silver case is worn. Hallmarked Birmingham, but year obliterated. Case maker's initials: W. & H. (Walker and Hall).

137. Watch from case shown above. Case diameter 2½ inches overall. Dial with heavy bold figures. Hands gold plated. Side set hand setting. Case stamped Argentan. Movement 30-hour bar lever of Swiss type, but not so stamped. Minimum jewelling — escape wheel is unjewelled. It is fair to say that most of the other Goliath watches in my collection are fully jewelled and of good standard.

138. Mr. R. E. Phillips, who after his retirement at the age of 70, overhauled the majority of the watches in my collection.

139. Mr. Stanley Smith who guided my steps in the field of watch collecting. At one time Mr. Smith and Mr. Phillips worked side by side in the firm of T. R. Russell and Co. of Liverpool.